THE JAMES O'KELLY SCHISM IN
THE METHODIST EPISCOPAL CHURCH

The James O'Kelly Schism

in the

Methodist Episcopal Church

by

Charles Franklin Kilgore

CASA UNIDA DE PUBLICACIONES

Apartado Postal 97 Bis

México 1, D. F.

Primera edición:
Mayo de 1963.

Library of Congress
Catalog card number: 63-18914

Impresora Galve, S. A.—Callejón de San Antonio Abad 39.—México, D. F.

TABLE OF CONTENTS

TO

Gwen

whose "price is far above rubies"

PREFACE

The value of a study of the O'Kelly schism is seen in the light it sheds on the history of the Methodist Church and of the Restoration movement of Alexander Campbell and Barton W. Stone. The O'Kelly schism is illustrative both of the variety of religious experience in America and of the endeavor to restore in modern times the church as it was in the apostolic age. The purpose of this study is to present as objectively as possible the separation from the Methodist Episcopal Church and to ascertain the relationship between O'Kelly's movement and that of Campbell and Stone.

The manuscript was originally presented as a doctoral dissertation to the Faculty of the Division of Religion, Graduate School of Arts and Sciences, Emory University, Atlanta, Georgia. I am greatly indebted to Dr. James W. May for his expert guidance, to Dr. Walter B. Posey, Dr. William Mallard, and Professor John Lawson, who read the manuscript and offered many valuable suggestions, and to Mrs. Oma Johnson, Elon College, North Carolina, who made available rare editions of O'Kelly's works. I also wish to express my gratitude to my wife, Gwen, for her invaluable encouragement and assistance, and to Carla and Karen, whose cooperation made their father's task easier.

Union Seminary
Mexico City, Mexico
January, 1963

CHAPTER I

THE ORIGINS OF THE SCHISM

John Wesley's message of "Christianity in earnest" was
first brought to America by Irish immigrants. Robert Strawbridge, from County Leitrim, Ireland, settled in Maryland
between 1760 and 1766 and preached to his neighbors in his
frontier cabin. As an itinerant preacher, he traveled in Maryland, Delaware, Pennsylvania, and Virginia, forming Methodist societies and "raising up" young preachers who assisted
in the expansion of the work. While Strawbridge was planting
Methodism in Maryland, other Irish immigrants were establishing the cause in New York. Philip Embury, a lay preacher, and his wife, along with several other families, came to
New York in 1760 from County Limerick, Ireland. Embury at
first united with Trinity Lutheran Church, but in 1766 formed a Methodist society in his home. Captain Thomas Webb,
an officer in the British army, joined the group in 1767 and
greatly strengthened it by his leadership and financial assistance. The Methodist forces in America were also strengthened
by the coming of Robert Williams and John King. Williams,
a member of the Irish Conference, came with Wesley's reluc-
tant permission, but on his own responsibility.[1] With impa-
tient zeal, he sold his horse to pay his debts, and set off for

[1] William W. Sweet, *Methodism in American History* (New York,
1933), pp. 49-58.

the ship to America with a "loaf of bread and a bottle of milk, and no money to pay his passage." [2] An Irish friend paid his passage, and Williams arrived in New York in 1769. After assisting Embury in New York and Strawbridge in Maryland, Williams preached in Virginia and North Carolina. John King, an English lay preacher, arrived in Philadelphia in 1769 and offered his services to the Methodist society there and later worked with Strawbridge in Maryland.[3]

Thus, Methodism had already established a foothold in America when Wesley's first official missionaries, Richard Boardman and Joseph Pilmoor, arrived in 1769. Boardman was the first "General Assistant," or Wesley's personally appointed supervisor of American Methodism. Two other missionaries, Richard Wright and Francis Asbury, arrived in 1771.[4] During the ocean voyage, Asbury had examined his motives for going to the New World. "To gain honour?" he asked himself. "No, if I know my own heart. To get money? No: I am going to live to God, and to bring others so to do." [5] Asbury served as General Assistant in 1772 but was replaced by Thomas Rankin, who arrived in 1773. When Rankin returned to England in 1778, Asbury again became General Assistant.[6]

Some of the preachers were too independent to submit readily to the discipline imposed by Wesley's representatives. Strawbridge was fiery and energetic and though unordained, administered the sacraments in spite of Asbury's objection. He was a thorn in the flesh to Asbury, and Asbury remarked at his death that "the Lord took him away in judgment because he was in a way to do hurt to his cause. . . ." [7] This spirit of

[2] Jesse Lee, *A Short History of the Methodists, in the United States of America* (Baltimore, 1810), p. 27.
[3] Sweet, *Methodism in American History*, pp. 58-59.
[4] *Ibid.*, pp. 59-64
[5] Francis Asbury, *The Journal and Letters of Francis Asbury*, ed. Elmer T. Clark (Nashville, Abingdon Press, 1958), I, 4.
[6] Sweet, *Methodism in American History*, pp. 68-93.
[7] Asbury, *Journal and Letters*, I, 60, 411.

independence caused Rankin, at the first conference of the American preachers at Philadelphia in 1773, to complain of the lack of discipline which prevailed. Drawing up rules to enforce a more rigid order, the conference strictly instructed the preachers to avoid administering the sacraments of baptism and the Lord's Supper, and urged the people, especially those in Maryland and Virginia, to receive the sacraments at the Established Church.[8]

Wesley was also concerned about the reluctance of the preachers to submit to discipline. On March 27, 1771, he wrote to Joseph Pilmoor to inquire if Robert Williams and John King were of a "teachable spirit," and if they cooperated with him. Wesley entreated John King to "pray for an advisable and teachable temper! By nature you are very far from it: you are stubborn and headstrong. Your last letter was written in a very wrong spirit. If you cannot take advice from others, surely you might take it from Your affectionate brother." [9] Robert Williams' anti-clericalism also disturbed Wesley. He noted, for instance, that a general love for the gospel had obtained in Manorhamilton, Ireland, until "simple" Robert Williams "preached against the Clergy." [10] Wesley urged the American preachers to act in "full union with each other" and not to let bitterness or anger creep in among them. As there would always be those who would set one man against another, they were to give such men "no countenance" and to "ferret them out and drag them into open day," marking them for what they were. If the preachers would work together, they could "overturn America." [11] The Methodists, indeed, were to "overturn America" or at least ultimately to exert

[8] *Minutes of the Annual Conferences of the Methodist Episcopal Church, 1773-1828* (New York, 1840), I, 5.
[9] John Wesley, *The Letters of the Rev. John Wesley, A. M.*, ed. John Telford (London, 1931), V, 232; VI, 167.
[10] John Wesley, *The Works of the Rev. John Wesley, A. M.* (London, 1866), III, 343.
[11] Wesley, *Letters*, VI, 57, 142-143.

a strong influence as the largest Protestant denomination, but this was not before they were to suffer some setbacks at the hands of dissident minorities who followed in the tradition of independence of Strawbridge, Williams, King, and the native preachers. One such dissident faction was led by an Irishman, James O'Kelly.

O'Kelly was born in 1735 of Irish ancestry, although it is not known whether he was born in Ireland or Virginia.[12] O'Kelly certainly called Virginia his native country.[13] Nothing definitely is known of his education, and he himself said that he was an utter stranger to classical education.[14] He belittled the use of Greek and Latin and said that while they might be useful in some occupations, in the church they were merely ornamental.[15]

O'Kelly married Elizabeth Meeks in 1759; and they settled in Chatham County, North Carolina, where O'Kelly owned a farm and a mill. Two sons were born to their marriage. In 1774, a Methodist circuit was formed which extended from Petersburg, Virginia, into North Carolina. In a revival which began in the region, Mrs. O'Kelly and one of the sons were converted, and O'Kelly shortly afterward.[16] O'Kelly joined the Methodist societies and became a lay preacher. The first mention of O'Kelly in the minutes of the annual conferences is in the record of the Virginia conference, where he is listed as remaining on trial in 1778. From 1779 to 1784, he traveled the New Hope, Tar River, Mecklenburg, Brunswick, and Sussex circuits. When the Methodist Episcopal Church was organ-

[12] Wilbur E. MacClenny, *The Life of Rev. James O'Kelly* (Indianapolis, Religious Book Service, 1950), pp. 11-16.

[13] James O'Kelly, *Essay on Negro-Slavery* (Philadelphia, 1789), p. 19.

[14] James O'Kelly, *The Author's Apology for Protesting Against the Methodist Episcopal Government* (Hillsboro, N. C., 1829), p. 65.

[15] James O'Kelly, *Letters From Heaven Consulted* (Hillsboro, N. C., 1822), p. 23.

[16] Peter J. Kernodle, *Lives of Christian Ministers* (Richmond, 1909), pp. 1-2.

ized at the Christmas Conference in Baltimore in 1784, O'Kelly was ordained an elder. He served as a presiding elder in southern Virginia from 1785 to 1792, with as many as twenty-eight preachers at one time under his supervision.[17] During this period, he became one of the most influential of the Methodist preachers.[18]

During the American Revolution, O'Kelly was captured by the Tories, but he refused to swear allegiance to the king. Released by the Tories, he subsequently enlisted in the Colonial army and served in two campaigns. O'Kelly is said to have been a friend of Thomas Jefferson, and there is a tradition that Jefferson had O'Kelly preach to Congress on two occasions.[19]

As an influential preacher, O'Kelly played a leading role in the controversy over the administration of the ordinances in 1779. At least in principle, the Methodist societies were considered to be a part of the Church of England, and Methodist preachers were only lay preachers. The Methodist people depended on the Episcopal clergy for the administration of baptism and the Lord's Supper. The Methodist preachers in Virginia, nevertheless, believed that they should have the right to administer the ordinances. O'Kelly says that a "murmuring" arose among the people and Southern preachers with respect to the ordinances because the "old church had corrupted herself." [20] Because of what was believed to be the "wickedness" of the Episcopal clergy, the Methodists wanted their own preachers to administer the ordinances.[21] Furthermore, because of the Revolution, there were few Episcopal ministers to whom

[17] *Minutes, 1773-1828*, I, 9-45.
[18] *Dictionary of American Biography* (New York, Charles Scribner's Sons, 1928-1958), XIV, 7.
[19] Milo T. Morrill, *A History of the Christian Denomination in America* (Dayton, Ohio, 1912), pp. 17, 114.
[20] O'Kelly, *Apology*, p. 4.
[21] William Guirey, *The History of Episcopacy, in Four Parts, From Its Rise to the Present Day* (n.p., n.d.), p. 257.

the people might go for the sacraments. The Southern preachers met in Fluvanna, Virginia, May, 1779, and appointed
a committee to ordain ministers. They believed that if God
had called them to preach, He had also called them to administer baptism and the Lord's Supper. The members of the
committee first ordained themselves and then proceeded to
ordain other preachers. The newly ordained ministers returned to their circuits and began to administer the sacraments.[22]

Asbury assembled the Northern preachers at Baltimore,
April, 1780. The conference disapproved the step which the
Southern preachers had taken in Virginia and decided that
they were no longer to be accounted as in connection with
Wesley and the Northern preachers. The conference appointed
a committee, consisting of Asbury, Freeborn Garrettson, and
William Watters, to inform the Virginia conference of this
action and to receive their answer. The required condition of
reunion was that the Southern preachers suspend the administration of the sacraments for one year and then all should
meet together in Baltimore.[23] Asbury, Garrettson, and Watters
met with the Southern preachers at the conference in Mana-
kintown, Virginia, to consider the matter. The conference could
not reach an agreement, and it seemed that all efforts at
reunion would fail. O'Kelly and John Dickins then proposed
that they should present their grievances to John Wesley: "We
proposed that Francis lay our grievances before Wesley and
that there should be a suspension of the ordinances until we
could receive counsel from him." [24] The Virginia conference
agreed to the proposal; but because of the struggle then going
on between Britain and the colonies, Wesley did not reply

[22] Lee, *A Short History of the Methodists*, pp. 67-69.
[23] *Minutes, 1773-1828*, I, 12-13.
[24] O'Kelly, *Apology*, p. 5. Nicholas Snethen later contended that
it was Asbury who made the proposal to lay the grievances before Wesley. See Snethen, *A Reply to an Apology for Protesting Against the
Methodist Episcopal Government* (Philadelphia, 1800), p. 8.

until the war was over.[25] The issue was settled in the Christmas Conference of 1784 when the Methodists were organized into a separate church and the preachers were ordained.

New political conditions resulting from the American Revolution led Wesley to take matters into his own hands and to ordain ministers for the Methodist work in America. As an elder in the Church of England, Wesley was convinced that he had scriptural authority to ordain, since, in his opinion, elders and bishops were the same order in the New Testament. Accordingly, he ordained Dr. Thomas Coke as superintendent and Richard Whatcoat and Thomas Vasey as elders. Coke was an elder in the Church of England, and Whatcoat and Vasey were Methodist preachers. On September 10, 1784, Wesley wrote to the American Methodists informing them that he had appointed Coke and Asbury as joint superintendents and Whatcoat and Vasey as elders.[26] "We perceived the counsel given in the circular letter to be good," O'Kelly observed, "because we are directed to follow the scriptures and the primitive church: and to stand fast in our liberties. Seeing we were free from the power of kings and bishops." [27] The American preachers assembled in Baltimore, December 24, 1784, and organized the Methodist Episcopal Church.[28] Asbury was ordained as deacon, elder, and superintendent, on successive days; thirteen preachers were ordained as elders.[29]

According to O' Kelly, the name adopted by the new church, "The Methodist Episcopal Church," did not set well with some, since Wesley had told them that episcopacy was not apostolic. "But Thomas [Coke] explained it away, by that

[25] O'Kelly, *Apology*, p. 5.
[26] Wesley, *Letters*, VII, 238.
[27] O'Kelly, *Apology*, p. 9.
[28] For a discussion of whether Wesley intended for the American Methodists to organize a separate church, see John A. Faulkner, *Burning Questions in Historic Christianity* (New York, 1930), pp. 207-232.
[29] Lee, *A Short History of the Methodists*, pp. 94-95.

8 CHARLES FRANKLIN KILGORE
8 CHARLES FRANKLIN KILGORE
indefinite term, 'Methodist Episcopacy' - - We had episcopacy, but no bishops." [30] O'Kelly misrepresented John Wesley's position in regard to the episcopacy. Wesley did not reject episcopacy or say that it was not apostolic. He believed the episcopal form of church government to be scriptural and apostolic.[31] It is true that he considered the uninterrupted succession a "fable." [32] He regarded the episcopal ministry, however, as the token of continuity with the ancient church.[33]

Although Wesley had appointed Asbury and Coke as superintendents, Asbury refused to serve unless elected by the American preachers. Asbury claimed that he was unanimously elected by the Christmas Conference.[34] O'Kelly denied that this was true. According to O'Kelly, Coke and Asbury were superintendents by virtue of appointment by Wesley. He asserted that "Thomas and Francis were our superintendents, as president elders; according to John's appointment. But they were not elected by the suffrage of conference, although it is so written in the book of discipline." [35]

The issue is difficult to resolve since no minutes of the Christmas Conference of 1784 are extant. In the minutes of the conference for 1785 an account is given of the formation of the Methodist Episcopal Church. These minutes state that the Methodists decided to become an episcopal church, "making the episcopal office elective, and the elected superintendent, or bishop, amenable to the body of ministers and preachers." [36]

[30] O'Kelly, *Apology*, p. 9.
[31] John Wesley, *Wesley's Standard Sermons*, ed. Edward H. Sugden (London, The Epworth Press, 1956), II, 139.
[32] Wesley, *Letters*, VII, 284.
[33] See John Lawson, *Methodism and Catholicism* (London, S.P.C.K., 1954), pp. 15-18.
[34] Asbury, *Journal and Letters*, I, 474.
[35] O'Kelly, *Apology*, p. 9.
[36] *Minutes, 1773-1828*, I, 22. The early *Minutes* are not entirely trustworthy, as they were revised by Asbury. See Guirey, *History of Episcopacy*, p. 287, and John J. Tigert, *A Constitutional History of American Episcopal Methodism* (Nashville, 1904), p. 222.

The *Discipline* for 1784 states that no person shall be ordained superintendent without the consent of a majority of the conference.[37]

Nicholas Snethen called O'Kelly's denial of Asbury's election a "notorious falsehood." According to Snethen, from the time of the Christmas Conference of 1784 until 1792, no one ever denied that Asbury had been elected. How was it, he asked, that a matter of such importance was concealed for such a long time? Why had not O'Kelly and others used this in their disputes with Asbury before?[38] That Coke and Asbury were also appointed by Wesley did not alter the case. To elect superintendents was one of the main reasons for calling the conference of 1784. Snethen gave a statement by Edward Dromgoole, Ira Ellis, William Watters, LeRoy Cole, and John Hagerty to the effect that they were members of the conference, and could testify that Asbury was elected by unanimous vote.[39]

In an attempt to reconcile the different opinions as to whether Asbury was elected or not, Guirey argues that the conference agreed to the plan proposed in Wesley's letter. Snethen considered this an election, while O'Kelly did not.[40] Drinkhouse, after considering the evidence, came to the same conclusion. The conference of 1784 agreed to receive Asbury and Coke as superintendents. Thus, to Asbury, this was an election; to O'Kelly, it was not.[41] The selection of Coke and Asbury was more a ratification of Wesley's proposal than it was an election.

The Christmas Conference agreed to obey Wesley in matters

---

[37] *Minutes of Several Conversations between the Rev. Thomas Coke, LL. D., the Rev. Francis Asbury and Others....* (Philadelphia, 1785), p. 11.

[38] Snethen, *A Reply to an Apology*, p. 9.

[39] Nicholas Snethen, *An Answer to James O'Kelly's Vindication of his Apology, Etc., and an Explanation of the Reply* (Philadelphia, 1802), pp. 9-10.

[40] Guirey, *History of Episcopacy*, p. 314

[41] Edward J. Drinkhouse, *History of Methodist Reform* (Baltimore, 1899), I, 289.

relating to church government: "During the Life of the Rev. Mr. Wesley, we acknowledge ourselves his Sons in the Gospel, ready in matters belonging to Church-Government, to obey his Commands." [42] O'Kelly, however, objected to this and went back to his district dissatisfied with the form of government which had been adopted. [43]

A further indication of O'Kelly's dissatisfaction with Methodist polity as it had been established at the Christmas Conference is seen in his opposition to Wesley's appointment of Richard Whatcoat as superintendent. Wesley, in a letter to Coke, September 6, 1786, directed that Whatcoat be appointed joint superintendent. [44] When Coke met Asbury in Charleston, Coke told him of Whatcoat's appointment and Asbury approved of it. So did the Charleston conference. [45] When the appointment was discussed at the Virginia conference, however, O'Kelly vigorously opposed it. His reasons were: (1) the free people of America were jealous of the "European heads" of the Methodist Episcopal Church, (2) Whatcoat was too young, (3) he had not been in America long enough, and (4) two heads would produce two bodies. [46] O'Kelly believed that a successful fight against Whatcoat's appointment was necessary if the American preachers were to free themselves of Wesley's authority. If this fight should be lost, he wrote to a friend, April, 1787, then

---

[42] *Discipline*, 1784, p. 3.

[43] O'Kelly, *Apology*, p. 10.

[44] Wesley, *Letters*, VII, 339.

[45] Snethen, *A Reply to an Apology*, p. 9. The regular Annual Conferences had not yet been organized. Before 1796, the "district conferences," varying in number from year to year, were regarded as sessions of a single yearly conference, opening at one place and adjourning at another. Asbury traveled from conference to conference, presenting the business matters before each group. At the end of the year, the *Minutes* were printed as if the business had been conducted at one time and one place. See Lee, *A Short History of the Methodists*, p. 118, and Tigert, *A Constitutional History of American Episcopal Methodism*, p. 221.

[46] O'Kelly, *Apology*, p. 11.

away to thy tents dear American preachers, after a long struggle thro' wars and famine, peril and naked, feeding a few frighted sheep driven about. You've no lot in the matter while our elder Brethren are planning beyond the water, we may be in our circuits waiting for further orders: and, for our consolation, they may say by us as the oppressors do by the slaves, "They have nothing to do but work, eat and sleep. We take care." [47]

O'Kelly challenged Wesley's directive by asking if Wesley thought that the American preachers were men of such low breeding that they were unfit to govern? Did he think they were novices, fond of popularity, who would fall into the snare of the devil? Did Wesley think that they were prone to revolt? Was there any political scheme in his proposal? In O'Kelly's opinion, preachers should have liberty to choose their masters.[48]

Coke, in the discussion during the Virginia conference, contended for Whatcoat's appointment; and because of the divergent views, Asbury proposed that the conference at Baltimore make the final decision. O'Kelly agreed, provided that the Virginia preachers be allowed to send a deputy to explain their position.[49]

When the conference assembled at Baltimore, May, 1787, Coke pressed for the acceptance of Whatcoat's appointment. The preachers strongly opposed it. The conference voted that Whatcoat should not be ordained superintendent and that Wesley's name should be removed from the American *Minutes*.[50] In his *Apology*, O'Kelly said that Asbury, with a few chosen men, in a "clandestine manner" expelled Wesley from the Methodist Episcopal Church.[51] Snethen defended Asbury,

[47] Letter in Asbury, *Journal and Letters*, III, 51-53.
[48] *Ibid.*, III, 53
[49] Guirey, *History of Episcopacy*, pp. 339-340.
[50] Snethen, *A Reply to an Apology*, pp. 12-13.
[51] O'Kelly, *Apology*, p. 12.

saying that Asbury did not make the motion nor did he advocate it. The motion was properly passed by the conference with a fair majority.[52]

On March 25, 1787, Asbury, accepting Wesley's authority, had written to Whatcoat that Wesley had appointed him as joint superintendent and that they would meet to make plans for their future work.[53] Wesley, however, blamed Asbury for the refusal to ordain Whatcoat as superintendent. He said that Asbury "flatly refused" to accept Whatcoat for the purpose for which he had sent him, and that Asbury "quietly sat by until his friends voted my name out of the American *Minutes*." [54] Wesley's name was reinstated in the *Minutes* of 1789 but not as before. The distinction was made that Wesley was the superintendent in England and that Coke and Asbury were superintendents of the Methodists in America.[55]

A rift was beginning to widen in Methodist ranks. The breach was evident in the controversy over the administration of the ordinances. Although the problem had seemingly been solved with the ordination of the preachers at the Christmas Conference of 1784, O'Kelly was dissatisfied with the new organization of the church. The spirit of independence and opposition to rule from above appeared in the controversy over Wesley's appointment of Whatcoat. This spirit was growing; and it was found mainly among the Virginia preachers, with O'Kelly the chief antagonist.

The controversy was intensified when the conferences of 1789 adopted a new form of government, the Council. This governing body was to be composed of the bishops and the presiding elders, and the decisions of the Council were to be unanimous. No resolution was to be binding on any district unless the conference of a district approved it. The idea behind

[52] Snethen, *A Reply to an Apology*, pp. 12-13.
[53] Asbury, *Journal and Letters*, III, 49.
[54] Wesley, *Letters*, VIII, 183.
[55] *Minutes, 1773-1828*, I, 32.

the Council was that it would be difficult and inconvenient to hold General Conferences regularly, and that it would be more expedient to have a Council composed of the bishops and presiding elders to govern the church.[56] Even as the Virginia preachers were voting their approval, O'Kelly realized that such a plan would bring disorder. He started to object, pointing out that what one district approved, another might reject. But "Francis jogged my elbow, and I ceased speaking." [57]

The first meeting of the Council was held in Baltimore on December 1, 1789.[58] According to O'Kelly, Asbury had already decided what course of action it should take. Asbury proposed that no preaching house be built without first obtaining the permission of the conference. O'Kelly opposed the motion because he believed that it was an invasion of the civil and religious liberties of the people. He discovered that Asbury was much displeased with his opposition. He reported Asbury as saying: "I can stay in *Baltimore* as long as you: and if I do not carry this, I will never sit in another council." O'Kelly secured a small amendment to the proposal and ceased his opposition. He told Asbury that the members of the Council were his tools and that he disliked being the tool of any man.[59]

At this meeting of the Council, the preachers were given a copy of a revised plan for the Council, which O'Kelly called the "new plan of government," and one characterized by a "very despotic nature." Nine elders were to act as the legislature, and the bishop would have the power of veto in the Council. The preacher who returned home with O'Kelly said that he would not travel under such a government. He soon married and ceased to itinerate, as did many others.[60]

---

[56] Tigert, *A Constitutional History of American Episcopal Methodism*, pp. 243-244.
[57] O'Kelly, *Apology*, p. 15.
[58] Lee, *A Short History of the Methodists*, p. 151.
[59] O'Kelly, *Apology*, pp. 16-17.
[60] *Ibid.*, p. 18.

Snethen, in his *Answer to James O'Kelly's Vindication of His Apology*, records a letter from a young preacher, which purports to relate what happened when O'Kelly returned. The writer of the letter reported that the minutes of the Council and a circular letter from O'Kelly arrived in the district before O'Kelly's return. The minutes said that O'Kelly agreed with everything, and the circular letter condemned everything. The young preacher was surprised at this but even more surprised when he saw O'Kelly in person, for the worst word O'Kelly could say against the bishop was too good. He charged the bishop with deceit and with being a mere savage, and no word was too bad to use about Asbury.[61]

When O'Kelly informed the Virginia preachers of the new plan of government, they were sorely displeased; but he assured them that they had the power to reject it in their district. O'Kelly felt that he had been deceived, and that the people had been imposed upon because they and the local preachers had not been consulted. He wrote to Asbury, asking for the space of a year in which to reconsider the matter, or, he suggested, if this were not possible, Asbury ought to relinquish his veto. If he refused, O'Kelly threatened to make trouble, and believed that it would be his duty to do so.[62] Asbury replied that he was greatly distressed by O'Kelly's letter and that he had never before received such a rebuff from any preacher in America. In his *Journal*, January 12, 1790, Asbury wrote:

> I received a letter from the presiding elder of this district, James O'Kelly; he makes heavy complaints of my power, and bids me stop for one year, or he must use his influence against me. Power! power! there is not a vote given in a conference in which the presiding elder has not greatly

[61] Snethen, *An Answer to James O'Kelly's Vindication of his Apology*, pp. 41-42.
[62] O'Kelly, *Apology*, pp. 18-19.

the advantage of me; all the influence I am to
gain over a company of young men in a district
must be done in three weeks; the greater part of
them, perhaps, are seen by me only at conference,
whilst the presiding elder has had them with him
all the year, and has the greatest opportunity of
gaining influence; this advantage may be abused;
let the bishops look to it: but who has the power
to lay an embargo on me, and to make of none
effect the decision of all the conferences of the
union?[63]

O'Kelly now began "to discover the rapid five-years growth
of 'A moderate Episcopacy.' Whereunto shall I liken it; it is
like unto a dwarf, whose head grows too fast for its body." [64]

When Asbury presented the new plan of government to
the Charleston conference in 1790, the conference rejected it.
Asbury, to win acceptance of the plan, altered the form in
which it had been approved in the Council. The altered plan
was then approved by the Charleston conference; but in North
Carolina, it was rejected. To win North Carolina's approval,
Asbury proposed another plan, which was nearly the same
in substance; and North Carolina accepted it. O'Kelly objected
to Asbury's changing the plan from conference to conference.
"By what authority," he asked, "did Francis (and a petty conference) alter, amend, extend, or abridge the resolves of an
ecclesiastical congress?" [65]

Asbury next attended the conference at Petersburg, Virginia, and presented the plan of government which had already
been modified by two conferences. O'Kelly observed that in
all the changes Asbury was careful to secure his power. When
the other preachers at the conference sought O'Kelly's advice,
he told them that they knew his mind on the subject, and that

[63] Asbury, *Journal and Letters*, I, 620; III, 81.
[64] O'Kelly, *Apology*, p. 19.
[65] *Ibid.*, p. 20.

they should assemble together for prayer. The next day, the conference rejected the plan. Asbury, amazed by the strong expression of opposition, said that they were out of the Methodist fellowship. O'Kelly commented:

> I was struck with astonishment to find that we were all expelled from the union, by the *arbitrary voice of one man:* for no offence, but voting according to our own *matured* judgment! We could have appealed to the people of our care, and produced our godly character; but ah! no; the *people* have not power to help themselves! Now I began to see![66]

Nor was there any point in appealing to Wesley, for Wesley himself had been cast out once before. O'Kelly wanted to present his side before the Northern conferences, but Asbury would not give him permission. The young ministers asked Asbury what they should do; and he told them that if they would accept him as bishop, he would station them in the district under the old plan.[67]

Snethen denied that O'Kelly and the young preachers were expelled. He admitted that Asbury, knowing that O'Kelly was behind the rejection of the plan, probably said some things which he later regretted. O'Kelly certainly took his usual station of presiding elder.[68] Who, asked Snethen, attended to O'Kelly's duties as presiding elder, and where and when was he readmitted to the Methodist connection if he was really expelled? [69]

O'Kelly wrote letters to the several conferences, presenting his side of the dispute, but these were to no avail. The new plan of government was adopted and a second meeting of the Council called. Asbury wrote to the Virginia preachers,

[66] *Ibid.,* pp. 20-23.
[67] *Ibid.,* p. 24.
[68] Snethen, *A Reply to an Apology,* p. 20.
[69] Snethen, *An Answer to James O'Kelly's Vindication of his Apology,* p. 21.

asking them to send a delegate to the Council. He assured them
that the Council would only be concerned with the "temporal-
ities" of the church. The Virginia preachers assembled in
conference to consider the matter. O'Kelly asked the conference what assurance they had that Asbury would keep his
word. He advised the conference to send an "affectionate" letter but no delegate, and the Virginia conference concurred.[70]
Asbury, apparently, was willing to consider a compromise:

> To conciliate the minds of our brethren in the
> south district of Virginia, who are restless about the
> council, I wrote their leader a letter, informing him,
> "that I would take my seat in council as another
> member;" and, in that point, at least, waive the
> claims of episcopacy; yea, I would lie down and be
> trodden upon, rather than knowingly injure one
> soul.[71]

With no delegate present from the Virginia conference, the
Council met for the second time in Baltimore on December 1,
1790, and endorsed the new plan of government. The Council
passed resolutions concerning the selling of books, the raising
of funds and subscriptions, and various matters pertaining to
Cokesbury College.[72] Although he was not present, O'Kelly
commented on the action of the Council. It appeared to him
that too much was said about money. He also objected to
Asbury's soliciting funds for a college. In O'Kelly's opinion,
God had sent the Methodist preachers to build up a holy,
simple-hearted people, not to build colleges.[73]

O'Kelly wrote a letter to Coke to obtain his help in the fight
against the Council, and he was successful in his efforts.[74] On
February 23, 1791, Asbury met Coke on his return from Eng-

---

[70] O'Kelly, *Apology*, pp. 24-26.
[71] Asbury, *Journal and Letters*, I, 649.
[72] Lee, *A Short History of the Methodists*, pp. 155-158.
[73] O'Kelly, *Apology*, pp. 27-29.
[74] *Ibid.*, p. 29.

land and found that he agreed with O'Kelly in regard to the
Council. Asbury remarked in his *Journal* that O'Kelly's letters
had reached London.[75] According to O'Kelly, Coke "withstood
Francis to the face; condemned his conduct. . . ." [76] Coke supported O'Kelly's request for a General Conference, and Asbury
acquiesced. "I felt perfectly calm," he wrote, "and acceded
to a general conference, for the sake of peace." [77] The purpose
of the General Conference was to consider the matter of the
Council.

Coke and Asbury attended the meeting of the Virginia
preachers in Petersburg. Coke told them that a General Conference would be called, and that the Council would stand
or fall by the decision of this conference. According to Guirey,
Coke said that he approved O'Kelly's conduct, and promised
that the treatment O'Kelly had received would not be overlooked but would be laid before the General Conference. Coke
assured O'Kelly that the General Conference would reject the
Council. If Asbury would not be satisfied with the government
as it had been before the Council, then they would contend for
a "republican government." [78] Wesley certainly would not
have agreed to such a proposal. "As long as I live," he wrote,
"the people shall have no share in choosing either stewards or
leaders among the Methodists. . . . We are no republicans, and
never intend to be." [79]

Coke hastened to England at the death of John Wesley;
but before leaving, he wrote to O'Kelly, May 4, 1791, urging
him to stand resolute in his opposition to the Council:

> You may depend on my being with you, God
> willing, at the General Conference. I think no step
> will be taken during my absence, to prevent the

[75] Asbury, *Journal and Letters*, I, 667-668.
[76] O'Kelly, *Apology*, p. 29.
[77] Asbury, *Journal and Letters*, I, 667-668.
[78] Letter in Guirey, *History of Episcopacy*, pp. 367-368.
[79] Wesley, *Letters*, VIII, 196.

General Conference; it would be so gross an insult on truth, justice, mercy, and peace, that it will not be, I think, attempted. If it be, and successfully, we will call a Congress. I expect you to be faithful. But as Mordecai said to Esther, think not with thyself that thou shalt escape more than others; for if thou altogether holdest thy peace at this time, then shall deliverance arise to the Jews from another place; but thou and thy father's house shall be destroyed. Oh, be firm, be very firm, and very cautious, and very wise, and depend upon a faithful friend in Thos. Coke.[80]

Asbury, however, attempted to bring about a reconciliation with O'Kelly, to whom he wrote:

Let all past conduct between thee and me, be buried, and never come before the Conference, or elsewhere, —send me the dove. I saw thy face was not towards me in all the council, therefore did not treat thee with that respect due to one who had suffered so much for the cause of truth and liberty.[81]

Asbury believed that he had succeeded in making peace with O'Kelly and wrote to Freeborn Garrettson, February 18, 1792, that all was unity in Virginia.[82] Events at the General Conference were to prove otherwise.

In the controversies which have been discussed, O'Kelly and his followers manifested a spirit of rebellion against authoritarian church government. The decision of the Fluvanna conference in 1779 to ordain ministers to administer the sacraments was an early indication of a desire to throw off restraint and to proceed on an independent course. The spirit of independence and the resentment against authority led to the rejection of Wesley's appointment of Whatcoat and to the

---

[80] Letter in O'Kelly, *Apology*, pp. 115-116.
[81] Asbury, *Journal and Letters*, I, 692; III, 104-105.
[82] *Ibid.*, III, 110.

removal of the pledge to obey Wesley in matters of church government. O'Kelly led the fight against the Council, since it concentrated power in the hands of the bishop and his appointees, the presiding elders. This desire for more democracy in the church was to lead to a division at the General Conference of 1792.

Chapter II

THE FORMATION OF A NEW DENOMINATION

The struggle between Asbury and O'Kelly was clearly leading to a climax. The issue between them was supposedly the powers of the Council; but the real issues, as events were to prove, were Asbury's power and the episcopal form of government. Both sides had marshalled their forces and were ready for action when the General Conference met in the Light Street Church in Baltimore, November 1, 1792, with Dr. Coke as president.[1] Under the rules adopted, a new rule or the repeal of an old one was to require a two-thirds majority, while to change an existing rule required only a majority vote. The conference also appointed a committee to expedite its business.[2] Asbury read the names of the members of the committee and asked if anyone objected to any of them. Although he was one of those chosen, O'Kelly felt from past experience that this committee was intended as a means of controlling the conference.[3] The new committee had the power to plan the agenda of the conference, and no business could be brought before the conference unless the committee had first considered it.[4]

Coke and Asbury met with the committee the first evening, and made some revisions in the *Discipline*. The next day, this

[1] Asbury, *Journal and Letters*, III,112.
[2] Lee, *A Short History of the Methodists*, pp. 177-178.
[3] O'Kelly, *Apology*, p. 31.
[4] Guirey, *History of Episcopacy*, p. 372.

action of the committee was presented to the conference. Some
of the members objected when they discovered that the burning question of the Council was apparently not going to be
considered.[5] Although Coke had promised O'Kelly his support
at the General Conference, he now sided with Asbury.[6] When
Coke tried to silence any mention of the Council, Richard Ivey,
a presiding elder, protested vigorously, raising the cry of "popery." O'Kelly, observing that the matter of the Council would
not be considered, and that the time would be spent in revising
the *Discipline*, proposed that the conference put aside all other
books and accept the New Testament as its only guide.[7] John
Dickens, the superintendent of the Methodist printing and book
business in Philadelphia, opposed the motion, arguing that the
Scriptures do not provide an explicit form of government.
He claimed that the Lord had left the precise form of church
administration to the decision of his ministers, according to
what is found suitable at different times and places. After a
debate, a vote was taken and O'Kelly's motion lost.[8]

O'Kelly then proposed to change the rule which gave the
bishop the right to make the appointments of the preachers.
He moved that if a preacher felt himself injured by his appointment, he could appeal to the conference. If the conference
approved his objection, the bishop would appoint him to another circuit.[9] A long and spirited debate followed the introduction of this motion. Since the motion concerned Asbury's
power, the bishop discreetly withdrew. He sent the following
letter to the conference:

[5] O'Kelly, *Apology*, pp. 31-33.
[6] Guirey advances the theory that Coke, disappointed in his hope of
securing power in England after Wesley's death and fearful of losing
his episcopal office in America, decided to side with Asbury and his party.
History of Episcopacy, pp. 369-370.
[7] O'Kelly, *Apology*, pp. 33-34.
[8] Guirey, *History of Episcopacy*, p. 373.
[9] *Journal of the General Conferences of the Methodist Episcopal
Church, 1792* (Cincinnati, 1899), p. 2.

Let my absence give you no pain —Dr. Coke presides. I am happily excused from assisting to make laws by which myself am to be governed; I have only to obey and execute. I am happy in the consideration that I never stationed a preacher through enmity, or as a punishment. I have acted for the glory of God, the good of the people, and to promote the usefulness of the preachers. Are you sure, that, if you please yourselves, the people will be as fully satisfied. They often say, "Let us have such a preacher;" and sometimes, "we will not have such a preacher —we will sooner pay him to stay at home." Perhaps I must say, "his appeal forced him upon you." I am one, ye are many. I am as willing to serve you as ever. I want not to sit in any man's way. I scorn to solicit votes. I am a very trembling, poor creature to hear praise or dispraise. Speak your minds freely, but remember, you are only making laws for the present time. It may be that as in some other things, so in this, a future day may give you further light.[10]

As the debate progressed, John Dickins moved that the issue be considered in two parts: (1) whether the bishop should appoint the preachers to the circuits, and (2) whether the preachers should be allowed an appeal. The first part carried unanimously. The question then arose as to whether the second part was a new rule or an amendment to an old one. The conference finally agreed that it was an amendment. This meant that the right of appeal needed only a majority vote, not a two-thirds vote.[11]

The debate centered around both the principle of authority and the judgment of the bishop in exercising that authority. O'Kelly believed that unless the absolute power of Asbury to station the preachers were curtailed, some of the best men

[10] Asbury, *Journal and Letters*, III, 112-113.
[11] Lee, *A Short History of the Methodists*, p. 179.

would be injured and excluded from the connection.[12] Asbury's defenders contended that the right of appeal would reflect on the "wisdom" and "goodness" of the bishop. They maintained that the bishop always made good appointments. But O'Kelly urged them not to attribute infallibility to the bishop, for Asbury had made many injudicious appointments. Asbury's defenders then wanted to know who had been injured. Rice Haggard, a young preacher from O'Kelly's district, answered that he knew of two preachers who had been badly treated by Asbury. At this, many cried, "He has impeached the bishop." Haggard responded that he had not meant it as an impeachment. O'Kelly said that if any further testimony were needed relative to Asbury's injuring anyone, he was one who had suffered.[13]

In opposition to O'Kelly's view, some said that if the right of appeal were granted, easy and wealthy circuits would be crowded with preachers, while the poor circuits would be left desolate.[14] Wesley himself had devised the appointive system and considered it essential to the preservation of the itinerancy. Furthermore, he never relinquished his assumed right to station the preachers. The right of appeal, some thought, would present many difficulties. If a preacher appealed and the conference approved it, the bishop would have to remove someone else to give place to the aggrieved preacher. The preacher who was thus displaced might then complain. The preachers might even complain about their second appointments.[15]

Henry Willis, a preacher from Philadelphia, protested against a balance of power, basing his arguments on church history. Stephen Davis, who was from O'Kelly's district,

[12] O'Kelly, *Apology*, p. 35.
[13] *Ibid.*, pp. 36-37.
[14] *Ibid.*, p. 38.
[15] Thomas Ware, *Sketches of the Life and Travels of Rev. Thomas Ware* (New York, 1840), pp. 218-222.

2080 9

thought that the arguments were badly founded and that in his opinion they had gone far into popery. Hope Hull, from Hartford, Connecticut, spoke in favor of the motion: "O heavens! are we not Americans! did not our fathers bleed to free their sons from the British yoke? and shall we be slaves to ecclesiastical oppression?"[16]

The debate continued until Monday night, November 5, when the vote was taken and the motion lost. Out of more than a hundred members, O'Kelly's group had only a small minority.[17] It may well be asked why the motion failed when at first the majority appeared to be for the right of appeal.[18] Thomas Ware, a participant in the debate, from Staten Island, New York, believed that if O'Kelly's motion had been managed differently, it would have been accepted. At first, Ware saw little that was objectionable in the right of appeal, but in the debate he heartily disliked the spirit of its advocates and the severity of their language. According to Ware, some said that "it was a shame for a man to *accept* of such a lordship, much more to *claim it....*" Those who would submit to this "absolute dominion must forfeit all claims to freedom, and ought to have their ears bored through with an awl, and be fastened to their master's door and become slaves for life." One said that to be denied an appeal was an insult to his understanding and a form of tyranny to which he would not submit. Those opposing the motion were more dispassionate in their arguments.[19]

After the vote was taken, O'Kelly and a "few true brethren" went to the home of a friend, and there spent a great part of the night "in groans and tears." The next day, he and his followers sent a letter to the conference, saying that

[16] O'Kelly, *Apology*, p. 38.
[17] *Ibid.*, pp. 37-38.
[18] Lee, *A Short History of the Methodists*, p. 179.
[19] Ware, *Sketches of the Life and Travels of Rev. Thomas Ware*, pp. 218-222.

they were withdrawing from the conference and from the
traveling connection.[20] Some of the young preachers, having
been converted under O'Kelly's ministry, were dismayed at
the defection; and the conference appointed a committee to
urge O'Kelly and his followers to return.[21] They refused to
do so. The members of the committee reported to the conference that they believed that God was with O'Kelly. Bit-
terly displeased with this report, Coke said that O'Kelly and
the others had broken their public faith since they had promised to abide by the decision of the conference. A member
arose and said that Coke was entirely wrong. Coke, with great
warmth, stoutly maintained that he was in the right, and
"offered to stake his salvation" on it. A member of the conference went to O'Kelly and told him that Coke had injured
his character. O'Kelly then wrote to Coke: "The slander is so
public, I earnestly desire *christian* satisfaction." It was Coke,
O'Kelly insisted, who had betrayed his trust. Previous to the
conference, Coke had promised O'Kelly help against Asbury;
but at the conference, he had deserted O'Kelly and sided with
Asbury. Coke replied that he would meet with O'Kelly and
the Virginia preachers that night and give satisfaction. At this
meeting, O'Kelly told Coke that he had treated him cruelly.
Stephen Davis then accused Coke of false assertions and profane
swearing. Coke then "confessed his sins, charging himself
with 'false zeal;' and in a very gentle manner, asked pardon
'ten thousand times.' " Privately, he asked O'Kelly on what
terms he would return. O'Kelly said that he would return if
the conference granted the right of appeal. Coke said that
this could not be done. On further consideration, O'Kelly regretted his answer for he knew that the adopted form of Methodist government was destitute of scriptural authority. It

---

[20] O'Kelly, *Apology*, pp. 39-40.
[21] Lee, *A Short History of the Methodists*, pp. 179-180.

was out of weakness that he had said that he would go back on such terms.[22]

O'Kelly then left for his home, accompanied by a few friends. Jesse Lee described his departure:

> Waiting in town a day or two longer, he and the preachers that were particularly influenced by him, set off for Virginia, taking their saddlebags, great coats, and other bundles on their shoulders or arms, walking on foot to the place where they left their horses, which was about twelve miles from town.

> I stood and looked after them as they went off, and observed to one of the preachers, that I was sorry to see the old man go off in that way, for I was persuaded he would not be quiet long; but he would try to be head of some party.[23]

As they traveled together, John Rice asked O'Kelly what he was planning to do. O'Kelly answered that he must preach the gospel wherever there was an opportunity, but that he had no intention of forming a separate party. What advice, then, would he give to those who would be converted under his preaching? O'Kelly relates that he responded that perhaps he would advise them to join the Methodists rather than to be without a church home. When asked if he would advise them to subscribe to a form of government which he knew did not have divine authority, O'Kelly admitted he did not know what to answer.[24]

Later that month, Asbury met with the Virginia conference; and at his suggestion, the conference agreed to allow the disaffected preachers to continue preaching. Since O'Kelly was "almost worn out," the conference acceded to Asbury's proposal to continue O'Kelly's annual stipend of forty pounds,

[22] O'Kelly, Apology, pp. 40-42.
[23] Lee, A Short History of the Methodists, p. 180.
[24] O'Kelly, Apology, pp. 42-43.

provided that he did not cause division among the brethren.[25]
O'Kelly looked upon this action as another example of Asbury's
unwarranted authority and his unscriptural power over the
people.

> If Francis gives a grant to any minister to preach,
> and administer among them, their doors must be
> open. Then, if Francis sends his authority to shut
> the doors against the same minister, none must open.
> This is "the power of the keys." [26]

O'Kelly accepted the offer of the pulpits but not of the
money. Later, Asbury sent O'Kelly ten pounds. O'Kelly considered this money a gift from Asbury,[27] though the Methodist officials considered it part of the salary authorized by
the Virginia conference.[28] The news spread that O'Kelly was
receiving support from the Methodists. An elder rebuked O'Kelly for preaching about church government, for the people
had no business with such knowledge. The elder then men-
tioned the money that O'Kelly had received. O'Kelly said that
surely they did not expect the money to be "hush money."
The people would ask, and he must teach. Doors were soon
closed to him, instructions were given that no one was to
publish his appointments, and the people were warned against
hearing him preach.[29]

O'Kelly and his followers met early in 1793 in Charlotte
County, Virginia, and drew up a petition with proposed
changes in church government and sent it to Asbury. The
bearers of the petition believed that Asbury treated it con-
temptuously.[30] Yet Asbury considered his attitude to be one
of quiet withdrawal from those who were unwilling to receive
him, and who thought they could do better service apart from

25 Asbury, *Journal and Letters*, I, 736.
26 O'Kelly, *Apology*, p. 43.
27 *Ibid.*, p. 44.
28 Snethen, *A Reply to an Apology*, pp. 34-35.
29 O'Kelly, *Apology*, p. 44.
30 Guirey, *History of Episcopacy*, pp. 378-379.

him. In his *Journal*, he wrote, "I have no time to contend, having better work to do: if we lose some children, God will give us more." Writing to Ezekiel Cooper, the presiding elder at Boston, Asbury expressed the hope that the division would not be as formidable as he feared and as O'Kelly boasted.[31]

The Methodists now began to erect defenses against O'Kelly. When O'Kelly drew up another petition on the evils of episcopal government, some of the Methodist local preachers warned their members that any who signed the petition would be expelled from the church. The people replied that there was no law to prevent their signing it, but the preachers pointed out that there was a rule in the *Discipline* against the "sowing of discord." [32] In 1792, a rule providing for the exclusion of those who sowed dissension by "inveighing against" either Methodist doctrine or discipline was added to the section of the *Discipline* dealing with the exclusion of "disorderly" persons. Additions to the *Discipline* in 1789 and 1792 reflected the growing dissension within the church. To the section dealing with the necessity of unity, a paragraph was added in 1789 which emphasized the evil consequences of division; and in 1792 a recommendation was added that the people read *The Causes, Evils, and Cures of Heart and Church Division*.[33] This latter work was a compilation which Asbury had made of Jeremiah Burroughs' *Heart Divisions, the Evil of our Times*, and Richard Baxter's *The Cure of Church Divisions*. Feeling "the pain of a partial separation" from some of his brethren, Asbury had been encouraged by reading these works and believed that they would be of "great service" to the Methodists.[34]

[31] Asbury, *Journal and Letters*, I, 752; III, 124.
[32] O'Kelly, *Apology*, p. 45.
[33] *Discipline*, 1789, p. 16; *Discipline*, 1792, pp. 38, 56.
[34] Francis Asbury, *The Causes, Evils, and Cures of Heart and Church Divisions* (Nashville, 1875), pp. vii-viii.

O'Kelly and his followers appointed a conference to meet at Piney Grove, Virginia, on August 2, 1793. The minutes of the conference show the attitude and purpose of the dissenters:

Quest. 1st. WHAT is the intention of the present meeting?

Ans. To confer together respecting our grievances as Preachers and Members of the Methodist Church!

Quest. 2d. Wherein do we consider ourselves aggrieved?

Ans. The Bishop claims such absolute power over the preachers, and the Preachers over the people, that the present form of Government, to us appears despotic, and of course unscriptural!

Quest. 3d. Do we resolve unless our grievances are redressed to leave the connection?

Ans. We feel ourselves under the painful necessity of so doing!

Quest. 4th. What shall be done in order to obtain redress?

Ans. We will address the Bishop, as an individual, at the District conference; and although he has not power himself to redress us, yet if we can obtain his consent to call a meeting on the subject as requested in our petitions, in order to form a permanent plan for peace and union, taking the Holy Scriptures for our guide —We will cheerfully wait.

Quest. 5th. Who are appointed to wait on the Bishop with the address, and make the report to our next meeting?

Ans. John Barker, Robert Walthal, and Thomas Goode!

Quest. 6th. When and where shall our next meeting be held?

Ans. On the 25th day December next, at the Manakin Town!

Quest. 7th. What is the intention of the said meeting?

Ans. 1st. To receive the answer of the Bishop!

> And 2ndly. To form such resolutions as may be
> thought necessary for the future.[35]

The purpose of the meeting which the conference wanted
Asbury to call would be to examine the episcopal form of government, to try it and amend it by the Scriptures. By this
means, O'Kelly hoped that a reunion would result. The conference appointed three delegates to carry the proposal to Asbury and then adjourned to await his answer. The meeting
reassembled at Manakin Town on December 25, 1793. Asbury's answer was that he had no power to call such a meeting. So far as O'Kelly was concerned, all hope of union was
lost. Asbury's reply sounded to him like the voice of Reho-
boam, who told the Israelites he would make their yoke
heavier.[36] Faced with the alternatives of "slavish subjection"
or separation, the conference unanimously chose separation.
The group formed a new religious body on a democratic basis:
"We formed our ministers on an equality; gave the lay-mem-
bers a balance of power in the legislature; and left the executive business in the church collectively." They called the new
church "The Republican Methodist Church." Within a few
days, one thousand Methodists joined the new church.[37] Methodist ministers, such as John Allen, Rice Haggard, and John
Robertson, united with O'Kelly.[38]

William McKendree, who later became a Methodist bishop,
left with O'Kelly but soon returned to the Methodist fold. As
a young preacher, McKendree had served a circuit under
O'Kelly's supervision from 1788 to 1792.[39] During this time,
McKendree was greatly influenced by O'Kelly, who used
every opportunity "to warn" McKendree of the threat posed

[35] Guirey, *History of Episcopacy*, pp. 379-380.
[36] I Kings 12:6-15.
[37] O'Kelly, *Apology*, pp. 45-48.
[38] *Minutes, 1773-1828*, I, 49.
[39] *Ibid.*, pp. 30-45.

to the church by the "bishop and his creatures." McKendree believed O'Kelly's charge that Asbury's pride and ambition would ruin the church because, as he wrote, "I then had and still have, a tender regard for the prosperity of Zion, and watched whatever I thought would injure her, with a jealous eye." Consequently, he refused to accept an appointment after the General Conference of 1792. Shortly afterward, however, Asbury met him and persuaded him to travel with him. As they traveled together, McKendree soon changed his opinion of the bishop and agreed to accept an appointment to the Norfolk circuit. McKendree became one of the most vigorous defenders of Methodist episcopacy and waged a campaign from 1820 to 1824 against the "Reformers," who agitated for the election of presiding elders by the Annual Conference.[40]

The members of the Manakin Town conference decided to look upon their form of organization as tentative, and to settle on a permanent organization at the next general meeting. Accordingly, the Republican Methodists, as they temporarily called themselves, met in Surry County, Virginia, on August 4, 1794. The proceedings of the conference were open to all. It was soon evident that a minority was dissatisfied with the form of organization. To attain unity, the conference appointed a committee of seven to draw up a plan of government and to present it to the conference the next day. When the committee was unable to reach an agreement, one of its members proposed that they put aside every manuscript and use only the Scriptures. He claimed that this was the right method, for the primitive church had used only the Scriptures. However, since the people had not been taught to search the Scriptures for church discipline, the committee drew up an outline of principles to be used as a guide. This outline asserted that (1) any number of Christians, united in love with Christ as

[40] Robert Paine, *Life and Times of William McKendree* (Nashville, 1869), I, 43-66, 139-142, 407-464.

their head and center of union, constitutes a true Church; (2) in the primitive church, there were twelve apostles who possessed the keys of the kingdom and were authorized by Christ to write His last will and testament; and (3) after the death of those elders who possessed extraordinary powers such as prophecy and speaking in tongues, only one order of ministers existed in the early church.[41]

After the committee made its report the following day, the conference unanimously proclaimed Jesus to be the head of His people and renounced all human institutions in the church as a form of "popery" not fit for the discipline of Christian souls. As "free citizens in the land of Columbia" and as servants of Christ, the conference ordained elders according to what it believed to be the divine order. The candidates appeared before the conference, and the qualifications as given by the apostle Paul were read and explained.[42] The members were given the right to say whether these men were their choice. Those chosen were ordained with the words:

> In the name of our Lord Jesus Christ, by the authority of the holy scriptures, with the approbation of the church, and with the laying on of the hands of the presbytery, We set apart this our brother, to the holy order and office of an Elder, in the church of God: In the name of the Father, and of the Son, and of the Holy Ghost —Amen.[43]

Thus O'Kelly and his followers began to build the church upon what they believed to be the true basis. They rejoiced to find that the primitive church government, which came down from heaven, was republican.[44] To complete their adherence to this "apostolic order," the members of the con-

[41] O'Kelly, *Apology*, pp. 48-49. Also see Hebrews 9:15-17.
[42] I Timothy 3:1-7.
[43] O'Kelly, *Apology*, pp. 50-51.
[44] *Ibid.*

ference adopted the name "Christian." Rice Haggard suggested the name because it was given to the church by divine
authority.[45]

The new church grew rapidly in Virginia and North Carolina. O'Kelly had preached in this area for sixteen years and
was one of the most influential men among the Methodists,
and many of them followed him into the new church. In some
places, the entire membership joined the disaffected group.[46]
Devereux Jarratt, an Episcopal clergyman, noted the divisive
spirit at work among the Methodists. "O'Kelly does great things
in the divisive way and I dare say he will make Asbury's
Mitre set very uneasy on his head, so as to give sensible pain
to his heart, and it may be to such a degree that he may
sincerely wish Dr. Coke had never given him a Mitre at
all." [47] The Methodists were disturbed by this loss of their
members. "It was enough," Jesse Lee commented, "to make
the Saints of God weep between the porch and the altar. . .
to see how 'The Lord's flock was carried away captive,' by
that division." [48] By 1809, the movement had spread until
there were twenty thousand members in the Southern and
Western states.[49] The greatest growth was in southern Virginia and North Carolina, where O'Kelly continued to make
his home until his death in 1826.[50]

During the same period, two other movements, which later
merged with O'Kelly's group, arose independently. One movement, under the leadership of Elias Smith and Abner Jones,
was among the Baptists in New England.[51] The other was

[45] Rice Haggard, *An Address to the Different Religious Societies on
the Sacred Import of the Christian Name* (Nashville, Disciples of Christ
Historical Society, 1954), p. 13.
    [46] Lee, *A Short History of the Methodists*, pp. 204-205.
    [47] Asbury, *Journal and Letters*, III, 138 n. 55.
    [48] Lee, *A Short History of the Methodists*, p. 205.
    [49] *Herald of Gospel Liberty*, I (1808-1809), p. 43.
    [50] MacClenny, *The Life of Rev. James O'Kelly*, p. 228.
    [51] *Herald of Gospel Liberty*, I (1808-1809), pp. 1-2.

THE FORMATION OF A NEW DENOMINATION
35

among the Presbyterians in Kentucky, under the leadership
of Barton W. Stone.[52] Both groups rejected the Calvinism of
their tradition and adopted the New Testament as their only
rule of faith and practice. The three groups each learned of the
existence of the others through itinerant ministers, by corres-
pondence, and from the journal, *Herald of Gospel Liberty*,
published by Elias Smith in New England and circulated in
other sections. When the members of the three groups learned
of the similarity of their doctrine and practice, they desired
fellowship and unity with each other. On December 8, 1808,
the *Herald of Gospel Liberty* published a letter by William
Lanphier, who identified himself as a member of the Christian
Church which had members in Virginia, North Carolina, South
Carolina, Georgia, Tennessee, Kentucky, Ohio, and Pennsylvania. He had heard of Smith's group from a friend in Philadelphia who gave him five copies of the *Herald*. Lanphier
believed that the Chrisian Church would be glad to give Smith
the right hand of fellowship. William Guirey, a Methodist
minister who joined O'Kelly's movement in 1797, also wrote
to the editor of the *Herald*, saying that he would be glad to
unite with the Christians in New England if there was no
episcopacy or Calvinism among them. On May 27, 1809, ministers from Virginia, North Carolina, and South Carolina
assembled in Virginia and sent greetings to their Christian
brethren in New England. They rejoiced to know that the
"Christians" in New England (1) accepted Christ as the only
head of the church, (2) took the New Testament as the only
rule of faith and practice without any addition or changes,
and (3) wore the name "Christian." Three ministers in New
England returned their greeting, saying that they were brethren in the kingdom.[53]

[52] Barton W. Stone, *History of the Christian Church in the West*
(Lexington, Kentucky, The College of the Bible, 1956), pp. 1-53.
[53] *Herald of Gospel Liberty*, I (1808-1809), 1, 32, 39, 43, 65, 87, 95.

The leaders compared their work to the rebuilding of the walls of Jerusalem by Nehemiah. Guirey wrote to Elias Smith:

> Your allusion to the building of the wall, in the days of Nehemiah, is beautiful and correct; for each man did build the wall before his own house. Our brethren in Virginia, and in the lower part of North Carolina, and in South Carolina, in Kentucky, and in Philadelphia, builded without knowing any other persons were engaged in the work; they were entirely ignorant of each other, and our brethren in New England builded without knowing any thing of the brethren in the south. "This is the Lord's doings, and it is marvellous in our eyes." [54]

Although the churches looked upon themselves as one, denominational consciousness came slowly. Many members were suspicious of organized, delegated conferences. They feared that individuals and churches would lose their independence. Nevertheless, the safeguarding of the ministry and the churches gradually outweighed this fear. Conferences were organized as voluntary associations, and no minister or church was required to join. A conference was composed of ministers in good standing and of delegates from churches. It could make recommendations for the churches, but it could not legislate for them. To preserve the good name and integrity of the brotherhood, a conference could, if necessary, exclude ministers and churches. Qualifications for membership varied from conference to conference, but a general requirement was the possession of a Christian character. Although a conference usually respected the declarations of another conference, each was free to act independently of the others.[55]

The leaders of the Christian Church were slow in organiz-

[54] *Ibid.*, p. 66.
[55] Morrill, *A History of the Christian Denomination in America*, pp. 126-139.

ing a General Conference. The first General Conference met in Portsmouth, New Hampshire, in 1808, and intermittently in the following years.[56] The first General Conference with official delegates met in 1820.[57] After 1834, the General Conference met quadrennially.[58] The measures adopted by the General Conference were advisory only.[59]

The church split over slavery at the General Conference in 1854. A majority report said that slavery was an infringement on human rights. The Southern minority, however, said the right of private judgment was fundamental in the church, and that the South should be allowed to manage its own institutions.[60] The Southerners withdrew and formed the General Convention of the Christian Church, South, in 1856. The two groups reunited in 1894.[61] The Christian Church ceased to exist as a separate denomination when it united with the Congregational Church in 1931 to form the Congregational Christian Church.[62] This latter group merged with the Evangelical and Reformed Church in 1957 and is now called the United Church of Christ.[63] The Christian Church never grew large numerically. In 1926, before its merger with the Congregational Church, it numbered only 112,795 members.[64]

The conflict between the exponents of a more democratic

---

[56] John P. Barrett, ed., *The Centennial of Religious Journalism* (Dayton, Ohio, 1908), pp. 571-572.

[57] Morrill, *A History of the Christian Denomination in America*, pp. 140-141.

[58] Barrett, *The Centennial of Religious Journalism*, p. 572.

[59] Simon A. Bennett, *The Christian Denomination and Christian Doctrine* (Dayton, Ohio, n.d.), pp. 27-28.

[60] William A. Harper, *The Genius of the Christian Church* (Elon College, N. C., 1929), p. 34.

[61] Barrett, *The Centennial of Religious Journalism*, pp. 577-597.

[62] See Chapter IV for the relationship of O'Kelly's Christian Church to the present day Christian Church (Disciples of Christ).

[63] Benson Y. Landis, ed., *Yearbook of American Churches, 1959* (New York, National Council of the Churches of Christ in the U.S.A., 1959), p. 44.

[64] U. S. Department of Commerce, Bureau of the Census, *Religious Bodies: 1926* (Washington, 1929), II, 314.

church government and those who favored the episcopal system had resulted in a serious schism in the Methodist Episcopal Church. When O'Kelly and his followers failed in their
attempt to curb the powers of the bishop at the General Conference of 1792, they left the Methodist connection and organized a church which they considered to be both scriptural
and republican.

Chapter III

THE REASONS FOR THE SEPARATION

The Methodists and O'Kelly gave different interpretations of the separation which resulted in the establishment of a new denomination. O'Kelly maintained that he was not responsible for the separation from the Methodist Episcopal Church. He claimed that he had always been opposed to division, and continued among the Methodists in love and friendship as long as he could. They, he insisted, had shut their doors against him and driven him from their fellowship. What else was there for him to do but leave? The Methodists said that he had no business among them, to which O'Kelly's rejoinder was: "What, have no business among mine own children in the Lord; and my Master's family, where I have spent the prime of my life?"[1]

O'Kelly considered it his duty to speak out against the episcopal form of government. In times past, he observed, when Zion was overthrown by the ambition of bishops and of their creatures the priests, the people of God had accepted it in silence.[2] They, therefore, shared the blame with the corrupt clergy. The church was not to accept corrupt ministers or their doctrine.[3] The purity of the church should not be sacrificed for the sake of peace.[4]

[1] O'Kelly, *Apology*, p. 115.
[2] *Ibid.*, p. 69.
[3] O'Kelly, *Letters From Heaven Consulted*, pp. 37-38.
[4] O'Kelly, *Apology*, p. 72.

It was Asbury's tyranny, O'Kelly maintained, that caused the separation. Asbury preached against slavery and then subjected the church to tyranny. He removed Wesley's name from the *Minutes*, and then exercised a far more lordly and tyrannical power over the church than Wesley ever did. "Yea, his little finger has proved thicker than Wesley's loins." In his tyranny, Asbury did not follow the example of the apostle Paul, for "Paul did never exercise the authority that Francis doth. He did not lord it over their faith, nor send a minister but by his free consent. This is plain." Asbury was always careful to secure his power, a power which injured the church.[5]

Asbury had such power and influence that, in O'Kelly's opinion, he completely dominated the conference. The conference was not free because Asbury usually originated the laws. The preachers were men under his authority. The bishop was supposed to be amenable to the conference; yet the conference gave Asbury power to act as he saw fit. How could the conference punish Asbury in any legal way, O'Kelly asked, for using the power with which they had invested him? Even the method for bringing the bishop to trial for immoral conduct was impracticable. Three traveling elders had so to believe him guilty that they would prefer charges against him. They then had to secure the aid of six other ministers, together with whom they would constitute a committee to investigate the charges against the bishop. If the committee found him guilty, it could suspend him until the next General Conference.[6] O'Kelly objected that the approval of the laity did not have to be secured. In such a situation, the church could be injured. The ministers, O'Kelly argued, would be unlikely to execute justice, since they knew that they depended on the bishop for their bread.[7]

---

[5] *Ibid.*, pp. 13, 21, 35-36, 78, 98, 119.
[6] *Discipline*, 1792, pp. 17-18.
[7] O'Kelly, *Apology*, pp. 67-69.

O'Kelly was convinced that it was the episcopal system which enabled Asbury to act as a tyrant. The form of government which he resisted was "despotic, not free; human, not divine; changeable, and not permanent." [8] The spirit of episcopacy was power and pre-eminence. Recorded in Matthew 20 is an early manifestation of the episcopal spirit, in that two disciples wanted the chief seats in the kingdom. Jesus answered them according to their own folly when he said that they would drink of the cup of his affliction. There would be no lordly prelates in the gospel kingdom.[9] Diotrephes, who loved the pre-eminence, was an early example of the spirit of a bishop.[10]

The Scriptures gave no basis for episcopacy. To support his position, O'Kelly cited Acts 14:23, where Paul and Barnabas ordained elders in every church. Not a word was said about a superior order of bishops. The great conference recorded in Acts 15 was composed of apostles, elders, and people.[11] Elders were appointed to succeed the apostles in the care of the churches. Prelates who claimed pre-eminence should show their scriptural authority. Bishops and elders were the same in New Testament times.[12] Since Christ was king as well as redeemer, his subjects were bound to obey him in scriptural government.[13]

O'Kelly claimed that episcopacy started about fifty years after the time of the apostles. The elders became "wise above what was written" and changed the form of divine government. Presbyters began to form councils. In time, one of the members of the council became president and the others his

---

[8] *Ibid.*, p. 67.
[9] James O'Kelly, *The Divine Oracles Consulted: Or an Appeal to the Law and Testimony* (Hillsboro, N. C., 1820), pp. 19-20.
[10] O'Kelly, *Letters From Heaven Consulted,* p, 57. Also see III John 9.
[11] O'Kelly, *Apology,* pp. 81-82.
[12] O'Kelly, *Letters From Heaven Consulted,* p. 53.
[13] O'Kelly, *The Divine Oracles Consulted,* p. 31.

deputies. The president, who began to superintend cities and
provinces, was first called "senior," "apostolic father," "me-
tropolitan," and then "bishop." These men were humble at
first, but soon they began to act as legislators and sent out
canons or binding laws. The ambition of the bishops and "the
torpid subjection of the people, with the help of the bishop's
creatures, planted the seeds of popery. Episcopacy is the root
of popery; and *popery* is episcopacy in full bloom!" Some of
the ancient churches complained against the innovation but
were silenced by the inferior ministers. The people relinquished their right of judgment. They gave up their Bibles and
decided that it was safer to follow the bishop. This, in O'Kelly's
opinion, was exactly what happened in the Methodist Church.
"The writings of Francis in his book on divisions, his conduct,
and that of his elders among the Methodists, together with
the strange conduct of the good people, compared to this, an-
swereth like face to face in a glass!" The episcopacy originated
among the Methodists in 1787 when Asbury directed the
preachers to "title him Bishop." The *Discipline* of 1791 said
that Methodist episcopacy proceeded from Wesley. But Wesley was only an elder in the episcopal Church of England and
did not have the power to send letters of episcopal authority
to America.[14] O'Kelly overlooked the point that both Wesley and he believed that bishops and elders were the same
in the New Testament. Wesley, therefore, was consistent when
he ordained ministers for America.

Furthermore, O'Kelly insisted, ministers were not a separate order with special authority. They were only leading
and gifted members of the church. The New Testament did
not give different laws for the bishop, the elder, and the different orders. Instead, the New Testament taught that ministers were servants and not masters to be served. Jesus, in
humility, washed the disciples' feet; therefore, bow "ye haugh-

[14] O'Kelly, *Apology*, pp. 11, 62, 80-89.

ty prelates, and fall before the Lord thy God!"[15] The apostle Paul solemnly charged ministers to be humble and not to be puffed up with spiritual pride. The spirit of pride was the unclean episcopal spirit and was not of God. It would be a great day for the church when the ministers became humble, for one

> great deliverance shall be when the crown falls from the despot's head; when the white surplice, the black gown, the three-cornered caps, are all out of fashion, and the reverend clergy become the humble presbyters; it will effect such a change in church and state, that it may be called "a new heaven and a new earth, wherein dwelleth righteousness." [16]

In New Testament days, the itinerant and "located" ministers were equal co-workers. One was not above the other.[17]

Contrary to the "scriptural order," the *Discipline* gave itinerant preachers the right to expel members for immoral conduct or for breach of the bishop's rules.[18] When the apostle Paul gave a charge to the church of Christ to expel "wicked people," he charged the church collectively, not the pastor or the bishop.[19] Neither did Paul send out bulls to expel the false teachers among the Galatians. The power to expel rested in the church collectively.[20] Some might object that when private members judged the conduct of their brethren, they seldom did justice. This might happen at times; yet it was still the true order, for Scripture commanded, "Tell it to the church." [21] Some might also object that where there was no bishop to rule, the preachers neglected the work, as did John

---

[15] *Ibid.*, p. 108.
[16] O'Kelly, *Letters From Heaven Consulted*, p. 11.
[17] O'Kelly, *Apology*, p. 102.
[18] *Discipline*, 1792, pp. 55-57.
[19] I Corinthians 5:1-13.
[20] O'Kelly, *Letters From Heaven Consulted*, pp. 17, 28.
[21] Matthew 18:17.

Mark. The apostle Paul, however, did not expel Mark, but only refused to travel with him. The churches had power over the ministers, for they could suspend or expel them. Preachers were in subjection to God, to one another, and to the whole church. This was the "primitive order." [22]

Christ required His disciples to keep "corrupt doctrine" and "innovations" out of the church. Christians were told to hold fast to the truth and to cast error away. They were to obey preachers only insofar as they taught the truth. Otherwise, Christians would be obeying men instead of God. If preachers refused to follow the Scripture, then the lay members had the responsibility to follow it themselves.[23]

In the Methodist Episcopal Church, O'Kelly argued, the church had no voice in forming the rules by which she was governed. The government of the church was fully consolidated under one archbishop. No "located" minister, steward, leader, or lay member had a voice in the conference. This meant that they had no voice in forming the rules by which they were governed.[24] "Who," asked O'Kelly, "are these sitting in the temple as gods? And not one cent of power left the lay members?"[25] Preachers could be received on trial by the bishop, his deputy, or the conference, but not by the people. The governors of the people were chosen from among the preachers and by the preachers. The bishop exercised the power of veto over the ordination of the preachers. The presiding elders were chosen by the bishop and they remained in office at his discretion. The General Conference was an absolutist and despotic body, for the people had no restraining power. Since the members of the conference were not elected by the people, they were not responsible to the people. Yet

[22] James O'Kelly, *The Prospect Before Us. By Way of Address to the Christian Church* (Hillsboro, N. C., 1824), p. 76.
[23] O'Kelly, *Letters From Heaven Consulted,* pp. 49, 60.
[24] O'Kelly, *Apology,* pp. 92-93.
[25] O'Kelly, *The Prospect Before Us,* p. 51.

the canons which proceeded from this "ecclesiastical legislature" were binding on the whole church. The people were not allowed to object to any law.[26] Of all those whom the Lord sent out and of all those who assisted the apostles, none were so presumptuous as to write laws for the Lord's people. [27] Christ had set the church free and did not intend for her to dwell in bondage.[28]

If the Methodists wanted fellowship with O'Kelly, they must put aside their *Discipline*, and follow the form of government given by the apostles. "Let their episcopal dignity submit to Christ, who is the head, and only head of his church; and then we as brethren will walk together, and follow God as dear children."[29]

The loyal Methodists had a different view of the separation. To them, Asbury was not a tyrant; and the episcopal system was incompatible neither with liberty nor the Scriptures. They believed that the separation was due to O'Kelly's self-will and his desire to form a new party. They suspected that he was offended because the Methodist Church refused to publish his manuscripts, and that he was disappointed in his ambition to become bishop. Furthermore, they alleged that O'Kelly left because he feared a charge of heresy on the doctrine of the Trinity.

Nicholas Snethen, who wrote the official Methodist reply to O'Kelly's *Apology*, asserted that the purpose of the *Apology* had been to make Asbury appear an overbearing ecclesiastical tyrant, and to represent all Methodist preachers as participants in a system of ecclesiastical oppression. It was remarkable that O'Kelly criticized Asbury more than one hundred times in the *Apology*. No matter what happened, either at the Gen-

---

[26] O'Kelly, *Apology*, pp. 93, 99.
[27] O'Kelly, *The Prospect Before Us*, p. 75.
[28] O'Kelly, *Apology*, p. 112.
[29] O'Kelly, "A Plan of Union Proposed, etc.," *Herald of Gospel Liberty*, I (1808-1809), 39.

eral Conference or the district conferences, O'Kelly blamed
Asbury. It was unjust, Snethen argued, to blame Asbury for
everything done by the conferences. Those who attended knew
that motions were often passed against Asbury's wishes. Every
member had equal power, and all motions required a majority
vote for adoption. There was free debate, and every member
voted according to his own judgment. The General Conference
of 1792 appointed a committee to select and present the subjects of greatest importance to the conference. When the committee decided to revise the *Discipline*, each section was presented, debated, and either accepted or rejected by a majority
vote. If O'Kelly had a valid criticism of Asbury's administration, why, Snethen asked, did he not then bring a formal ac-
cusation against the bishop? He could have done this as well
as move that the conference make the New Testament the
sole criterion of church government. What more could Asbury
have done? He had agreed to hold a General Conference to
avoid division. He believed that the right of appeal would
destroy the itinerant system; yet he left the decision entirely
to the conference. Should Asbury, a bishop without veto over
the conference, have expelled all those who would not vote for
an appeal?[30]

Snethen was firm in his defense of Asbury. He could truth-
fully say that Asbury had labored more abundantly than all
the preachers. In spite of poor health, Asbury had traveled
"through almost all the inhabited parts of the United States"
to save souls. He endured more than the ordinary minister.
In addition, he had the general care of all the circuits and
stations. No one could rightfully accuse Asbury of seeking the
pomp and vanity of this world. If Asbury had made any
mistakes, they were of the head and not of the heart.[31]

O'Kelly, in Snethen's opinion, attacked the episcopal government as unscriptural, oppressive, and pernicious to religion in order to secure the affection of the Methodists, and to increase their indifference towards the other preachers.[32] What O'Kelly said about the episcopacy was a "heap of absurdities" around which he had raised "the mist of error and the fog of deception."[33] No one who knew Asbury and was not entirely controlled by prejudice could believe that he had directed the preachers to call him "bishop." What actually happened was that some of the preachers were disturbed over the use of the title "Reverend," and the conference of 1787 decided to let each preacher use his own judgment. Those who did not wish to use "Reverend" could simply use the designation of the office, whether bishop, elder, or deacon.[34] Moreover, if Methodist episcopacy had to be dated from the first mention of the title "bishop," it had to be dated from the Christmas Conference of 1784. Coke said in his sermon at Asbury's ordination that the bishops or superintendents had been elected. The American preachers, with the advice and consent of Wesley, agreed to organize a separate church and to call it the "Methodist Episcopal Church." Asbury was elected one of the bishops or superintendents. At this same conference, O'Kelly himself was ordained elder by the laying on of the bishop's hands.[35]

Wesley himself, Snethen reminded the disaffected, had recommended the episcopal form of church government. The American Methodists, however, introduced the practice of deciding all questions by majority vote. The preachers were encouraged to inform themselves about all questions and to discuss them in open debate. They voted their free and independent judgment. Asbury, as bishop, never claimed or exer-

---

[32] *Ibid.*, p. 53.
[33] Snethen, *An Answer to James O'Kelly's Vindication of His Apology*, p. 12.
[34] Snethen, *A Reply to an Apology*, pp. 10-11.
[35] Snethen, *An Answer to James O'Kelly's Vindication of His Apology*, pp. 12-13, 38.

cised the exclusive right to legislate for Christ's church.[36] The
bishop did not have a veto over the actions of a conference.
When, Snethen asked, did a bishop ever negate the actions
of a general or district conference? When did a bishop ever
nullify the election of an elder or deacon?[37] O'Kelly had tried
to represent old Methodism as destitute of all written rules and
the current Methodism as fettered with new rules to destroy
the people's liberty. The truth was that the changes which had
been made gave greater privileges to the local preachers and
lay members.[38]

The episcopal system, in Snethen's opinion, was not incompatible with liberty. For a community to exist, men had to
give up lesser privileges for greater.[39] O'Kelly had voluntarily
joined the Methodists and the itinerant connection. Any minister could leave the connection when he so desired. Snethen
here used the same argument Wesley used in the *Large Minutes.* There was an obligation to be a member of the church,
but not to be a member of the Methodist society within the
church. Those who wished to join the society did so on the
society's terms, or else could honorably leave.[40] This argument
does not apply in the same way to the church. Neither Wesley
nor Snethen argued that church membership was not essential.
Wesley argued that membership in a society within the church
was not essential, and Snethen, membership in a particular
denomination. If membership was voluntary, it was not "slavish
subjection." If O'Kelly did not believe in episcopal Methodism,
why did he join the connection in the first place and stay in
it so long? If he thought the presbyterian or congregational
form of church government was better, why did he not em-
brace such a church? The episcopacy was no more unfriendly

[36] *Ibid.*, pp. 22-23, 38.
[37] Snethen, *A Reply to an Apology*, p. 49.
[38] Snethen, *An Answer to James O'Kelly's Vindication of His
Apology*, pp. 27-28.
[39] *Ibid.*, p. 31.
[40] Wesley, *Works*, VIII, 300-301.

to liberty than Presbyterianism, Congregationalism, or Republican Methodism. The Congregational Church, supposedly the friend to religious liberty, was the established church in four states. As such, it sought support from the civil authorities. In New England, the Presbyterian and Congregational clergy had extensive livings and were as independent of the people as any of the Episcopal clergy. Furthermore, the episcopacy was not incompatible with piety. Pride, ambition, and the love of the world were not confined to episcopal churches. The Methodists ought not to be "terrified into ecclesiastical republicanism, by an imaginary dread of falling into popery." [41]

In Snethen's opinion, one reason why O'Kelly left was that he was head-strong. Some of his best friends saw in him a lamentable degree of self-will. While he was presiding elder, he ruled with a rod of iron; and people complained of his precipitate and violent excommunications. O'Kelly could not bear contradiction and left the Methodist connection rather than submit to the decision of the General Conference. [42]

Another reason why O'Kelly left was that he was disappointed in not being appointed bishop. If he had been promoted, he never would have attacked the episcopacy. What O'Kelly attributed to zeal for the Lord was really his own ambition and selfish purpose. O'Kelly was also disappointed in having his manuscripts rejected for publication. If Asbury had consented to O'Kelly's publication of his "crude indigested stuff," the Methodists would not have heard of the "attack on civil as well as religious liberty." [43] It was strange that one who refused to have fellowship with those who had books other than the Bible should complain of the Methodists' efforts to regulate the press so as to prevent a profusion of books. [44]

[41] Snethen, *A Reply to an Apology*, pp. 38-39, 58-60.
[42] Snethen, *An Answer to James O'Kelly's Vindication of His Apology*, pp. 23-29, 45.
[43] *Ibid.*, pp. 31, 39-42.
[44] Snethen, *A Reply to an Apology*, p. 43.

Still another reason prompting O'Kelly to withdraw from the Methodists was, in Snethen's opinion, his fear of being expelled for heresy. O'Kelly believed and propagated Unitarianism. Two of his itinerant preachers were convicted of heresy regarding the doctrine of the Trinity at a conference in May, 1792.[45] On arriving at Baltimore for the General Conference, one of the preachers related to O'Kelly that he had been examined for his beliefs. O'Kelly then became fearful that the conference would examine his own doctrine in regard to the Trinity.[46]

In short, it was the opinion of the Methodists that if O'Kelly had been given power, if his manuscripts had been approved for publication, if the preachers had accepted his views on the Trinity, he would then have been well pleased. Such a man as O'Kelly would not yield to bishops, councils, or conferences. "He must be head or nothing." [47]

Apart from the openly avowed reasons given by O'Kelly and the Methodists, there were factors which may have helped to bring about the separation. These factors were anti-Catholicism, anti-British sentiment, and the philosophy of Natural Rights of the Enlightenment.

Anti-Catholicism was an important factor in O'Kelly's day. Many Americans were steeped in antipapal prejudice. Roman Catholicism was regarded as a threat both to true Christianity and to civil liberty.[48] O'Kelly reflected this distrust of Rome. To him, the Methodist Episcopal system was nothing but "popery." He referred to the Methodist bishop as "prelate," "archbishop," and "holy see." [49] The church of Rome was corrupt

---

[45] *Ibid.*, pp. 32-33.
[46] Snethen, *An Answer to James O'Kelly's Vindication of His Apology*, pp. 43-45.
[47] *Ibid.*, p. 40.
[48] See Ray A. Billington, "The Roots of Anti-Catholic Prejudice," Chapter I, *The Protestant Crusade, 1800-1860* (New York, Rinehart and Company, 1952), pp. 1-31,
[49] O'Kelly, *Apology*, pp. 31-35.

and not to be imitated.[50] All human institutions in the church
were a form of popery. One such institution was the episcopacy.
Episcopacy was the root of popery and popery was episcopacy
in full bloom.[51] The primitive church gradually departed from
the divinely-given form of church government, and the result
was bishops and popes. The pope would smile if he heard the
Methodists advancing the idea that Christ had given men the
authority to govern the church.[52] To elevate the clergy and to
urge the church to trust in the judgment of pastors was a clear
mark of popery. O'Kelly considered Asbury's exercise of power
equivalent to that of the pope's: "Little did I once think, that
Francis would ever offer to exercise the Pope's keys!"[53] O'Kelly's
identification of Methodist episcopacy with the papacy is evident in a letter which he wrote shortly after his withdrawal:

> I only say no man among us ought to get into
> the Apostle's chair with the Keys, and stretch a
> lordly power over the ministers and Kingdom of
> Christ. 'Tis a human invention, a quicksand. . . . Boys
> with their Keys, under the absolute sway of one who
> declares his authority and succession from the Apos-
> tles —these striplings must rule and govern Christ's
> Church, as master workmen; as though they could
> finish such a temple. . . . I am a friend to Christ; to
> his Church, but not to prelatick government.[54]

In O'Kelly's opinion, episcopacy was inseparably linked with
popery.

Anti-British sentiment was also reflected in O'Kelly's attack on the episcopacy. Americans had just fought the War of
Independence, and antagonism toward the British naturally

---

[50] O'Kelly, *The Prospect Before Us*, p. 12.
[51] O'Kelly, *Apology*, p. 88.
[52] O'Kelly, *The Prospect Before Us*, pp. 51, 67-68.
[53] O'Kelly, *Apology*, p. 77.
[54] Letter to Jesse Nicholson in William W. Bennett, *Memorials of
Methodism in Virginia* (Richmond, 1871), p. 324.

carried over into religious affairs. O'Kelly observed that blood was the price paid for freedom from British tyranny. Why should the Methodists, therefore, still suffer under the authority of Asbury and Coke, both of whom were British subjects in their hearts? [55] What great attribute did these men possess, that the church had to bow to their caprice? Was it their wisdom, or the country from which they emigrated, or the principles of despotism which they brought with them? Asbury was born and reared in the land of kings and bishops, and brought authoritarian principles with him to America.[56] O'Kelly thus looked upon Asbury and episcopal Methodism as an extension of the Church of England and all its evils.[57] That O'Kelly was Irish explains some of his anti-British sentiment.

Another influential factor in the cultural and historical situation of O'Kelly's day was the Enlightenment philosophy of Natural Rights. The Enlightenment was to a large extent a protest against traditional reliance on authority. Man had natural rights to life, liberty, and the pursuit of happiness, and these could not rightfully be taken from him by the state. If the state invaded these, man had the right to revolt in the name of reason and justice. All men possessed the same rights, but the strong often took advantage of the weak. Hence, men had formed governments to enforce these rights. Corollary to this contract theory of the origin of civil government were the doctrines of the consent of the governed, popular sovereignty, and the right of revolution. These ideas could easily be used to justify more democratic forms of church government.[58]

[55] In fairness to Asbury and Coke, it should be pointed out that they called on George Washington, May 29, 1789, to congratulate him on his inauguration as president and to pledge their allegiance to the government. See Sweet, *Methodism in American History*, p. 120.

[56] O'Kelly, *Apology*, pp. 21, 58-59.

[57] See Arthur L. Cross, *The Anglican Episcopate and the American Colonies* (New York, 1902), pp. 226-240.

[58] Merle Curti, *The Growth of American Thought* (New York, Harper, 1951), pp. 103-118.

Of the philosophers advocating the theory of Natural Rights, John Locke enjoyed the widest popularity. His ideas of the relationship between church and state, liberty of conscience, and religion as primarily a personal concern, were influential in the thinking of Thomas Jefferson and James Madison.[59] Locke's doctrine of Natural Rights is clearly expressed in the following passage:

> Men being... by nature all free, equal, and inde-
> pendent, no one can be put out of this estate and
> subjected to the political power of another without
> his own consent. The only way whereby any one
> divests himself of his natural liberty, and puts on
> the bonds of civil society, is by agreeing with other
> men to join and unite into a community for their
> comfortable, safe, and peaceable living one amongst
> another, in a secure enjoyment of their properties
> and a greater security against any that are not
> of it.[60]

Thomas Jefferson gave the classic American expression of the philosophy of Natural Rights in the Declaration of Independence in which he asserted that governments received their just powers from the consent of the governed and that the people had the right to change their government.[61]

The ideology of Natural Rights was popularized through the mass circulation of pamphlets. Full expression was given to such ideas as the right of a people to determine their own fate, resistance to tyranny, and the glory of a struggle for liberty. Thomas Paine advocated these ideas in his pamphlets, *Common Sense* and *The American Crisis*. To Paine, America's

---

[59] William W. Sweet, *American Culture and Religion* (Dallas, SMU Press, 1951), pp. 38-39. Also see Gerald R. Cragg, *From Puritanism to the Age of Reason* (Cambridge, University Press, 1950), pp. 114-135.

[60] John Locke, *Two Treatises of Government* (New York, Hafner, 1947), pp. 168-169.

[61] Thomas Jefferson, "The Declaration of Independence," *We Hold These Truths*, ed. Stuart G. Brown (New York, Harper, 1941), p. 37.

cause was in a large measure the cause of all mankind because that which was in question were natural rights which all mankind possessed.[62]

The idea of liberty and equality as God-given rights which all men possessed was conducive to the development of the idea of equality in the churches. Furthermore, the right to resist and to alter governments lent encouragement to the idea of the members' right to revolt against despotic church government. In his attack on the episcopacy, O'Kelly joined the causes of civil and religious liberty.[63] He believed that the Methodists were erecting a throne for bishops at a time in history when others were fighting for liberty:

> Liberty is contended for at the point of the sword in diverse ways, monarchy, tyranny tumbling both in Church and Kingdoms, while our preachers are for erecting a throne for gentlemen Bishops in a future day, when fixed with an independent fortune they may sit and lord it over God's heritage.[64]

The close connection between the political situation and O'Kelly's revolt against the episcopacy is seen in the first name he chose for his church, the "Republican Methodist Church." In Virginia, it was considered advantageous to be a Republican.[65] O'Kelly reflected the philosophy of the Enlightenment when he declared that liberty was the birthright of all human beings.[66] America was an asylum for those who fled from tyranny. O'Kelly agreed with Patrick Henry that the people had a right to alter their government when they found it oppressive. Methodist government, unlike the civil government,

[62] Thomas Paine, *Selections from the Works of Thomas Paine* (New York, 1928), p. 3.
[63] O'Kelly, *Apology*, pp. 38, 50, 58.
[64] Letter to Colonel Williams in Bennett, *Memorials of Methodism in Virginia*, p. 325.
[65] Lee, *A Short History of the Methodists*, p. 203.
[66] O'Kelly, *Essay on Negro-Slavery*, p. 20 .

was a government imposed upon the people rather than receiving its authority from the people. Moreover, in the Methodist Episcopal Church, the legislative, judicial, and executive powers were all united in one body. In contrast, the civil government received its authority from the people; and the legislative, judicial, and executive powers were in three distinct departments. In O'Kelly's church, lay members had the balance of power, and executive authority was left to the local congregations.[67] In O'Kelly's opinion, a consolidated government was always bad.[68] Here again O'Kelly was in line with current political thought in Virginia, in this case, with Thomas Jefferson's advocacy of decentralized government.[69]

It may be argued that the basic reason for the separation was that O'Kelly had a primitivist doctrine of the church, which included the belief that the New Testament contained a fixed pattern which the church was to follow in all succeeding ages. He understood the pattern to contain a congregational form of government, with full autonomy for the local church and with a large degree of authority in the hands of laymen. O'Kelly believed that he was contending for the faith once delivered to the saints.[70] The true faith and order were first given to the church in Jerusalem, and from there the law and the government went forth into all the world that all the churches might believe alike and do alike. Paul taught that all the churches should follow the same rule and all mind the same thing.[71] Moses was charged to build the Old Testament church exactly by the pattern which was given to him on the mount. Christ built the new church according to the

[67] O'Kelly, *Apology*, pp. 47, 54.
[68] Letter to Jesse Nicholson in Bennett, *Memorials of Methodism in Virginia*, p. 324.
[69] See Stuart G. Brown, *The First Republicans* (Syracuse, Syracuse University Press, 1954), pp. 161-172.
[70] O'Kelly, *Apology*, p. 107.
[71] O'Kelly, *The Prospect Before Us*, p. 66. Also see Philippians 3:16, 17.

heavenly pattern, and the church must always conform to this pattern. In O'Kelly's view, "The sacred word is so fixed, and so well calculated by divine wisdom, that it completely serves for all nations and successive generations, till time shall be no more." [72]

The primitive church was guided first by the teaching of the Apostles and then by their writings.[73] These were read as the only rule book of faith and government.[74] The church was

> ordered to be subject to the apostles, who ruled and governed the churches by their sacred writings, which came from God through a pure channel; for they had the keys of the kingdom; therefore, that which they bound on earth, was, and is, bound in heaven.[75]

The New Testament contained a complete system for the faith and order of the church. Any addition was human corruption, defective, presumptuous, and dangerous to civil and religious society.[76] How then could ministers say that Christ did not give His church a set form of government and that He left it in the hands of men to govern the church, to alter and to change it to suit the times?[77] Christ was king and His subjects were bound to obey Him in scriptural government.[78]

The ancient church, however, departed from the primitive faith and order. "Innovations" and "false doctrines" corrupted the church. The addition of human rules to the sacred

---

[72] O'Kelly, *Letters From Heaven Consulted*, pp. iii, 17, 45-46. Also see Hebrews 3:2-6.
[73] O'Kelly, *Apology*, p. 87.
[74] O'Kelly, *The Divine Oracles Consulted*, p. 11.
[75] O'Kelly, *Letters From Heaven Consulted*, p. 49.
[76] O'Kelly, *The Divine Oracles Consulted*, p. 45.
[77] O'Kelly, *The Prospect Before Us*, p. 51.
[78] O'Kelly, *The Divine Oracles Consulted*, p. 31.

word brought about the rise of the episcopacy. When the church was established under Constantine and the preachers became great men, the churches grew rich, not knowing that they were miserable and poor.[79] O'Kelly lamented:

> See how far churches have wandered from divine orders, and do need a reform, a return to primitive purity.... This dreadful apostacy from the divine order, can never be too much lamented. These human inventions compose part of the hay, wood, and stubble that the walls of Zion are partly built of, that will go with the chaff into unquenchable fire. But the pure word abideth forever.[80]

In contrast to the fallen church, the true church had for its foundation the Apostles and prophets, with Jesus Christ the corner stone.[81] Christ was the only head of the church and its only lawgiver. There was only one order of ministers and these were equal co-workers. In this way, the true church stood fast in the liberty wherein Christ had made her free. It was strange that there were those who would part with their gospel liberty and, like Esau, sell their birthright.[82] To be like the primitive church, a church had to follow the royal standard, the word of God.[83] Apostolic doctrine was important and necessary for salvation.[84] Only those who believed and obeyed the truth would be saved.[85] Holy doctrine produced holy faith and holy faith produced a holy life.[86] Those who followed a crooked rule followed a crooked path and became crooked disciples.[87] Those who refused to submit to

[79] O'Kelly, *Letters From Heaven Consulted*, pp. 35, 39, 61.
[80] *Ibid.*, p. 18.
[81] Ephesians 2:20.
[82] O'Kelly, *Apology*, pp. 80, 97-100, 112.
[83] O'Kelly, *Letters From Heaven Consulted*, p. iv.
[84] O'Kelly, *The Divine Oracles Consulted*, p. 4.
[85] O'Kelly, *Letters From Heaven Consulted*, p. 30.
[86] O'Kelly, *Apology*, p. 107.
[87] O'Kelly, *Letters From Heaven Consulted*, p. 50.

the order and government of Christ would be destroyed with a sure destruction. The Lord desired a pure church, and the true church was composed of Christians who were gathered out of the multitude, baptized by one Spirit into one body of regenerated Christians. It had been foretold by the Lord's prophet: "Separate the precious from the vile. . . ." [88] It was his desire, O'Kelly told McKendree, to have a "no slavery, glorious" church.[89]

O'Kelly's conception of the primitive church as the standard for the church of all ages is seen in his use of the terms: "gospel order," "the days of truth," "the golden days of the church," "the heavenly pattern," "the pure apostolic order," "the good old primitive path," "the true order," "the primitive order," and "the good old way." [90] "Zion Restored to Order," a hymn which O'Kelly selected for his hymnal, expresses the hope for a restoration of the true church:

> From age to age has man been driv'n
> From wisdom's way the way to heaven;
> When gracious Lord wilt thou restore
> Thy Zion that she fall no more?
>
> Some thousand years are gone and pass'd
> Since from our Eden we were cast;
> And thus we've wander'd to and fro;
> O fix thy church to fall no more.
>
> We long to hear the Lord proclaim,
> I come my thousand years to reign;
> He then will set his Zion free,
> And sound the glorious jubilee.
>
> This sound shall favour every land,
> The preachers fly at his command;

[88] O'Kelly, *The Prospect Before Us*, pp. 10, 65.
[89] Paine, *Life and Times of William McKendree*, p. 65.
[90] O'Kelly, *Apology*, pp. 80, 111; *Letters From Heaven Consulted*, pp. 38-39, 46, 50, 58, 61; *The Prospect Before Us*, pp. 4, 68, 73, 76-77.

Enlarge their borders to and fro,
Such times were never seen before?

O hasten Lord that glorious day,
Come O Redeemer come away;
Come with the sceptre in thy hand,
And rule the church by thy command.

Then shall the lofty prelates know
We have no head but Christ below;
Himself the legislative God,
Who rules the kingdom by his word.[91]

O'Kelly's doctrine of the golden days of the church, the fall, and the restoration, was a primitivist conception like that of the Anabaptists in the days of the Reformation.[92]

The Methodists denied that the New Testament contained a detailed pattern of church government binding on later times, and affirmed that the form of government most suitable for the time and place was left to the judgment of the church. When O'Kelly moved in the General Conference of 1792 that the Methodists accept the New Testament as the only criterion, John Dickins opposed him, saying that the Scriptures did not give a sufficient form of government, and that the Lord had left the form of government to the judgment of the church.[93] Asbury also rejected the idea that the Scriptures alone were sufficient:

The apostle did not say the old Testament and the apostles are sufficient. They wrote forms of discipline for separate churches when cases of order and discipline called for such. These levellers say the scriptures are sufficient, granted, but in mass the Holy Word gives many changes in doctrine, we

[91] James O'Kelly, *Hymns and Scriptural Songs, Designed for the Use of Christians* (Raleigh, 1816), pp. 124-125.
[92] See Franklin H. Littell, *The Anabaptist View of the Church* (Boston, Starr King Press, 1958), pp. 46-108.
[93] Guirey, *History of Episcopacy*, p. 373.

only select from Scripture for doctrine, and for discipline in epitome or very small selections. If these levellers were consistent why not only the scriptures, and quit preaching or any comment at all.[94]

In Asbury's opinion, O'Kelly's doctrine led to anarchy:

> It is an open attack upon every reformed church upon articles and confessions of faith and on Convocations, General Assemblies, Synods, all associations or meetings of ministry of every order. They are not fifth monarchy men that would not set up the kingdom of Christ but anarchy men.[95]

Snethen contended that it was necessary for any church to draw up rules for its organization. Any denomination would dissolve if every member acted independently of his brother. This was as true of other denominations as it was of the Methodist Episcopal Church. To follow the Bible only would not work:

> It is vain to argue against human heads, and human institutions, and to recommend the bible only, as a standard to remedy the evil; for every man has an equal right to explain the bible for himself; and without explanation, it is a mere dead letter, which cannot be brought into effect: this will evidently appear, if we recur to facts.[96]

How, asked Snethen, would differences of opinion be reconciled? Without a guide or final authority, confusion would result. Every denomination had to decide upon some plan to explain controverted texts and to carry their deliberations into execution. The Holy Ghost had not intended that the Scriptures be used alone:

[94] Asbury, *Journal and Letters*, III, 415-416.
[95] *Ibid.*, III, 417.
[96] Snethen, *A Reply to an Apology*, p. 54.

> Had the Holy Ghost designed the scripture for
> a system of discipline and government in the church
> without the agency of human wisdom, or human
> prudence, one would be inclined humbly to conjec-
> ture, that he would have given it eyes, and ears,
> and a voice, that he might see, and hear, and deter-
> mine all complaints and difficulties in the church.[97]

Snethen did not mean to attribute infallibility to the church
or to condemn all who did not agree with her. He declared
that the Methodists believed in toleration. They did not try
to expose the governments of other churches. They could
admit that there were martyrs and saints in all churches,
whether Congregational, Presbyterian, or Episcopalian. The
duty of a Methodist preacher was to save souls. He was
not to show how fallen the church was but how fallen the
people were. Snethen here used another argument from Wesley, who said that "seceders" showed their hearers how fallen
the church and ministers were, but the Methodists showed
their hearers how fallen they were themselves.[98] According
to Snethen, preachers and people had been reared Episcopa-
lians; and they were attached to that form by tradition and
sentiment.[99] However, the Methodists were willing to improve
their polity if improvement were called for. Thus, William
Spencer wrote to John Robinson, who had left with O'Kelly:
"If there are defects in our Government, we are still improv-
ing, and often meeting together, to see what amendments
can be made for the better. Our Church Rules are not like
the laws of the Medes and Persians. . . ." [100]

If any one form of church government was more scriptural than others, it was the episcopal. Coke and Asbury de-

---

[97] Ibid., p. 55.
[98] Wesley, Works, VIII, 309.
[99] Snethen, A Reply to an Apology, pp. 55-57.
[100] Letter of William Spencer to John Robinson, November 14, 1809,
in Asbury, Journal and Letters, III, 422.

fended episcopacy in the explanatory notes which they prepared for the *Discipline* of 1796. These notes consisted partly of scriptural proofs of Methodist doctrine and rules and partly of expositions of the *Discipline*. Prepared at the request of the General Conference of 1796, the notes received the implied sanction of the General Conference of 1800, which directed that they be printed and bound with the *Discipline*. In these notes, Coke and Asbury maintained that any church had the right, if it so desired, to choose the episcopal plan of government. Wesley, the "most respectable divine since the primitive ages, if not since the time of the apostles," had recommended the episcopal form to his societies in America and had consecrated Coke for the office of bishop that the "episcopacy might descend from himself." Being "peculiarly attached to the laws and customs of the church in the primitive times of Christianity," Wesley preferred the episcopal form of government, since the "primitive churches universally followed the episcopal plan." [101] Coke and Asbury invoked the name of Wesley and the example of the primitive church in defense of Methodist episcopacy.[102]

Asbury was especially interested in episcopacy because to him it was necessary to the preservation of the itinerant system. He believed the itinerancy would soon cease if the bishop's right to station the preachers were curtailed.[103] When Asbury pleaded for episcopacy, he was not pleading for bishops who walked on "stilts of practical pride and worldly-mindedness," but for itinerant bishops, who "planted and watered" churches. The fall of the church occurred, in Asbury's opinion, in the second century when the bishops became

[101] For a discussion of whether there was a universal church order in the New Testament age, see Burnett H. Streeter, *The Primitive Church* (New York, 1929), pp. 69-100.

[102] Robert Emory, *History of the Discipline of the Methodist Episcopal Church* (New York, 1844), pp. 281-339.

[103] *Ibid.*, p. 293. Also see Peter G. Mode, *The Frontier Spirit in American Christianity* (New York, 1923), pp. 123-135.

"local" and ceased to itinerate. The primitive order, as it was revealed in the Acts of the Apostles, was the same as the "traveling apostolic order and ministry" which was found in the Methodist Episcopal Church.[104]

Snethen saw the episcopacy vindicated in the success of the Methodists. Where, asked Snethen, are the societies which O'Kelly and his brethren had established? Where are their converts, the seal of their ministry? Perhaps they had not had enough time. In the seven years since the separation, they had spent their time in exposing the evils of episcopacy and "opening the eyes of deluded people." When they had written a few more *Apologies*, perhaps they would turn their attention to evangelism. God had abundantly blessed the work of the Methodists in America. The last year (1799) had witnessed an outpouring of the Spirit which had never been experienced before. Snethen did not argue that the success which God had given to their ministry was a proof of their infallibility, but he did affirm that if the Methodists were as corrupt as O'Kelly said they were, God would not bless them.[105]

In summary, O'Kelly maintained that he left the Methodist Episcopal Church because the episcopal form of government was unscriptural and oppressive. The New Testament contained a pattern of church government which the church was to follow in all ages, and this pattern was congregational and democratic. In his view of church government, O'Kelly was deeply influenced by anti-Catholicism, anti-British sentiment, and the philosophy of Natural Rights. The Methodists contended that O'Kelly left because he was head-strong and would not submit to duly constituted authority. They charged that he was disappointed in his ambition to be bishop and in his desire to publish his manuscripts. Furthermore, he feared a charge of heresy regarding the doctrine of the Trinity. The

---

[104] Asbury, *Journal and Letters*, III, 475-492.
[105] Snethen, *A Reply to an Apology*, pp. 60-62.

Methodists felt that the form of church government was left to the judgment of the church, and that if any one form was more scriptural than others, it was the episcopal. As a sign of God's approval of their ministry, they cited the success which had attended their labors. The basic reason for the separation was a difference of opinion in regard to church government. O'Kelly believed in a congregational form of government, and the Methodists believed in episcopacy.

Chapter IV

O'KELLY AND THE RESTORATION MOVEMENT

O'Kelly taught that the pattern for the government of the church should be sought in the New Testament alone. Another movement, originating a few years later, was also interested in this same idea of restoring "primitive Christianity." This was the Restoration movement led by Alexander Campbell and Barton W. Stone. Earl West, in the *Search for the Ancient Order*, writes of various groups in the early nineteenth century which sought to restore primitive Christianity. He lists O'Kelly along with Stone and Campbell.[1] Historians of both O'Kelly's denomination and of the Restoration movement have considered Stone as one of their founders. Milo Morrill, a historian of O'Kelly's Christian Church, names seven men as the early leaders. He includes Stone but not Campbell. Morrill believed that Stone was a deserter when he joined Campbell's movement. He looked upon Stone's followers as members of O'Kelly's church and therefore considered it disastrous that most of the "Christians" in Kentucky and Tennessee followed Stone's lead and united with Campbell.[2] It is the purpose of this chapter to study the teachings of O'Kelly, Stone, and Campbell to determine the relationship of the men and their movements to each other.

[1] Earl West, *The Search for the Ancient Order* (Nashville, Gospel Advocate Company, 1949), I, xi.
[2] Morrill, *A History of the Christian Denomination in America*, pp. 15-64, 297-305.

O'Kelly, Stone, and Campbell were anti-Calvinist, since they rejected the doctrines of election, predestination, and total depravity.[3] O'Kelly believed that God was willing for all men to be saved.[4] He pointed to the example of the apostle Peter, who by a vision, was fully persuaded that salvation was for all.[5] At the Judgment, the Lord would clear himself of the unjust charge that he had unconditionally elected a few to salvation, and unmercifully condemned the greater part of the human race before they were born. There would be no talk of partial election and of sinners condemned by arbitrary power, for the Lord would make righteous judgments. The saints, as they witnessed the judgments of Christ, would be able to say "amen." They could not say this if the great majority were condemned by divine decree, merely because they were not of the elect.[6] In the Scriptures, predestination and election refer to the coming of Christ, and to his birth among the Jews. God decreed to give a Saviour to the world. He predestined the Saviour's generation according to the flesh. The Lord kept a chosen line of holy men in succession, such as Abel, Enoch, Noah, and Shem. In course of time, God chose Abraham, Isaac, and Jacob; and the Jews became an elect nation. The Calvinists thought they were part of the elect family, but they did not have part or lot in the history of the chosen people. The Calvinists, being Gentiles, were descendants of Japheth, and were no part of the elect people.[7] O'Kelly overlooked the point that the Calvinists, in claiming they were of the elect, did not mean that they were part of the Israel "after the flesh," but of the New Israel, the church. He did realize, however, that the word "Israel" can be used

---

[3] Although these doctrines are associated with Calvinism, other Christian groups have also taught them.

[4] O'Kelly, *Letters From Heaven Consulted*, p. 38.

[5] O'Kelly, *The Divine Oracles Consulted*, p. 50. Also see the Acts of the Apostles 10:9-35.

[6] O'Kelly, *The Prospect Before Us*, pp. 42, 60.

[7] O'Kelly, *Letters From Heaven Consulted*, pp. 11-12, 30.

in two senses, for he went on to say that after the coming of Christ, the elect were those who obeyed Him. Election was of grace and grace appeared to all. Those who came to the light became the elect; those who refused remained reprobates.[8] O'Kelly also rejected the doctrine of the final perseverance of the saints. There was no absolute assurance of salvation. He cited the example of fallen angels in Jude 6 to show the danger of falling from grace. O'Kelly warned young converts not to join a church which believed that Christians could not fall from their first justification.[9]

God had given free will to men, setting before them life and death, blessing and cursing. Man, though fallen, was free to choose.[10] Men were on probation, and there would be no virtue if man served God as a slave. The earth was man's place of trial. O'Kelly also rejected the idea of a limited atonement. Christ by His life made possible a general resurrection and by His death, a general redemption. Christ tasted death for everyone.[11] He suffered greatly, and those who said He suffered only for a few elect were attempting to lighten the burden which He bore.[12]

Stone was also anti-Calvinist and said that during his student days his spiritual life declined as a result of the systematic study of Calvinism. Previously, the Bible was the only theological book he had studied. He came to the conclusion that Calvinism was among the "heaviest clogs" on Christianity, and viewed the revivals as almost ruined by partisan Calvinists. The Presbyterian, Methodist, and Baptist preachers had all joined together and were preaching free salvation for all by faith and repentance. The sticklers for orthodoxy

[8] O'Kelly, *The Divine Oracles Consulted*, p. 54.
[9] O'Kelly, *Letters From Heaven Consulted*, pp. 42, 58.
[10] *Ibid.*, pp. 30-31.
[11] O'Kelly, *The Prospect Before Us*, pp. 46, 50, 71. Also see Hebrews 2:9.
[12] O'Kelly, *The Divine Oracles Consulted*, p. 43.

writhed under such doctrines but kept quiet, hoping that the converts would become Presbyterians. But when they saw the Baptists and Methodists gaining converts, they raised the cry of alarm.[13]

Stone had wrestled long with the doctrines of election, predestination, and depravity as taught in the Westminster Confession of Faith. He related his struggle in his autobiography:

> Often when I was addressing the listening multitudes on the doctrine of total depravity, their inability to believe —and of the necessity of the physical power of God to produce faith; and then persuading the helpless to repent and believe the gospel, my zeal in a moment would be chilled at the contradiction. How can they believe? How can they repent? How can they do impossibilities? How can they be guilty in not doing them? Such thoughts would almost stifle utterance, and were as mountains pressing me down to the shades of death.[14]

By reading the Scriptures, Stone became convinced that God loved all men and was willing for all to be saved. Men persisted in unbelief when it was within their power to believe. Stone rejoiced in his discovery of this "glimpse of faith of truth, [which] was the first divine ray of light, that ever led my distressed, perplexed mind from the labyrinth of Calvinism and error, in which I had so long been bewildered. It was that which led me into rich pastures of gospel-liberty." Stone also rejected the doctrine of a limited atonement. Jesus had died for all men, and salvation was offered to all.[15]

Campbell considered Calvinism one of the evils which plagued Christianity. He believed that only those who actually

---

[13] Barton W. Stone, "A Short History of the Life of Barton W. Stone, Written by Himself," in *Voices From Cane Ridge*, ed. Rhodes Thompson (St. Louis, The Bethany Press, 1954), pp. 42-44, 63-76.

[14] *Ibid.*, p. 61.

[15] *Ibid.*, pp. 63, 75.

and voluntarily sinned would be punished. Although man was greatly depraved, he was not under an invincible necessity to sin.[16] Man was free to make his own choice, for

> every man, in reference to spiritual and eternal blessings, shall certainly and infallibly have his own choice. Therefore, life and death, good and evil, happiness and misery, are placed before man as he now is, and he is commanded to make his own election and take his choice. Having chosen the good portion, he is then to "give all diligence to make his *calling* and *election* sure." [17]

O'Kelly, Stone, and Campbell also agreed on the doctrine of Christian perfection. O'Kelly believed that the Christian had to seek cleansing of all filthiness of the flesh and spirit and seek perfect holiness in the fear of God. A Christian should believe in the doctrine of perfection and seek after it. He was to walk by faith in a holy, obedient life.[18] O'Kelly defined Christian perfection as perfect love to God and good will to all men. A Christian could attain perfection, and Stephen was such a man.[19] The word of God, abiding in a man, was like seed which bore good fruit. Grace changed the sinner.[20] The Christian who carefully followed the Spirit was changed from glory to glory.[21] This growth in holiness was a preparation for heaven. All those who entered heaven were a "prepared people for that place, holy, pure in heart, and heavenly minded." [22] The Christian should never forget that faith without works is dead. To feel the comfort of the Spirit was not

[16] Alexander Campbell, *The Christian System* (Cincinnati, Standard Publishing Co., n.d.), pp. 4-5, 29.

[17] *Ibid.*, p. 33.

[18] O'Kelly, *Letters From Heaven Consulted*, pp. 26-27, 34.

[19] The Acts of the Apostles 6:5-15.

[20] O'Kelly, *The Divine Oracles Consulted*, pp. 9-10, 48.

[21] O'Kelly, *Letters From Heaven Consulted*, pp. 26-27, 34.

[22] O'Kelly, *The Divine Oracles Consulted*, p. 25.

enough.[23] Christians had to add more of every virtue to their faith, for they would be judged by their works.[24]

Stone also believed in striving after perfect holiness. He rejected the idea of imputed righteousness to enforce the argument that the merits of Christ did not free man of the obligation to love God with his whole heart and his neighbor as himself.[25] Religion without righteousness was to no avail.[26] Campbell conceived of sanctification as a holy character as well as a holy state. It was the duty of Christians to perfect holiness in the fear of the Lord, and Christians needed that holiness without which no one would see the Lord. The Holy Spirit was the author of this holiness. The Spirit, working in Christians, brought forth the fruit of love, joy, peace, long-suffering, gentleness, goodness, fidelity, meekness, and temperance. Thus, Christians were the sons of God in fact as well as in name.[27]

In regard to the doctrine of the church, Stone and Campbell agreed with O'Kelly that the primitive church was the standard for the church of all ages. The church had fallen, and there was a need to restore her to her former glory. Stone believed that those who departed from the precepts and example of the early church departed from the true foundation of the Apostles and prophets, and from Jesus Christ, the chief corner stone. The systems of men had corrupted the church for fifteen centuries.[28] Campbell regarded his work as an effort to restore primitive Christianity:

> Tired of new creeds and new parties in religion, and of the numerous abortive efforts to reform the reformation; convinced from the Holy Scriptures,

[23] O'Kelly, *Essay on Negro-Slavery*, p. 29.
[24] O'Kelly, *Letters From Heaven Consulted*, pp. 26, 49, 53.
[25] Stone, *History of the Christian Church in the West*, pp. 43, 46.
[26] Stone, *Voices From Cane Ridge*, p. 74.
[27] Campbell, *The Christian System*, pp. 65-66.
[28] Stone, *Voices From Cane Ridge*, pp. 84, 121.

from observation and experience, that the union of
the disciples of Christ is essential to the conversion
of the world, and that the correction and improvement of no creed, or partisan establishment in Christendom, would ever become the basis of such a
union, communion and co-operation, as would restore peace to a church militant against itself, or
triumph to the common salvation; a few individuals,
about the commencement of the present century,
began to reflect upon the ways and means to restore primitive Christianity.[29]

Basic to the aim of the restoration of primitive Christianity
was the acceptance of the Scriptures as the only rule of faith
and practice. Although other Protestant groups professed to
follow only the Scriptures, O'Kelly, Stone, and Campbell
believed that the use of creeds and books of discipline vitiated
this principle. Indicative of O'Kelly's attitude was the Scripture he selected for the title page of his *Apology*: "Through
thy precepts I get understanding: thy word is a lamp to my
feet, and a light to my path." In O'Kelly's opinion, the Scriptures were sufficient to govern the church.[30] Christ did not
intend for His disciples to be governed by laws made by
uninspired and ungodly men.[31] The gospel law was a "royal
law" and was superior to "home-made laws." [32] Ignoring the
sufficiency of the Scriptures, kings and bishops had forced
laws and creeds on the people of God.[33]

Stone was another who decided to follow the Scriptures as
the only standard of faith and practice. In the light of the
gospel, he saw many errors in the Westminster Confession.
Stone withdrew from the authority of the Synod of Kentucky,
because it considered "human opinions" the standard of or-

[29] Campbell, *The Christian System*, p. 5.
[30] O'Kelly, *Apology*, p. 108.
[31] O'Kelly, *The Prospect Before Us*, p. 52.
[32] O'Kelly, *Letters From Heaven Consulted*, p. 50.
[33] O'Kelly, *Apology*, p. 83.

thodoxy. Under its jurisdiction, he could not enjoy the liberty of studying the word of God for himself.[34]

Campbell believed that the church should practice only that for which a "Thus saith the Lord" could be given, either in express terms of Scripture or by approved precedent of the apostolic church.[35] By a "Thus saith the Lord," Campbell meant a New Testament passage which could be cited to support a doctrine or practice. He advocated the slogan, "Where the Scriptures speak, we speak; where the Scriptures are silent, we are silent." [36] For Campbell, as well as for O'Kelly and Stone, the portion of Scripture that was binding on Christians was the New Testament. He regarded the Old Testament as inspired and authoritative before the coming of Christ. Christians could use the Old Testament as devotional literature but not as a standard of faith and practice. Nothing in the Old Testament, not even the Ten Commandments, was binding on Christians unless it was repeated in the New. In Campbell's view, all efforts to support such practices as infant baptism, tithing, establishment of religion by civil law, and observance of holy days, by an appeal to the Old Testament were "repugnant to Christianity, and fall ineffectual to the ground; not being enjoined or countenanced by the authority of Jesus Christ." [37] Campbell also chose to speak of Bible things by Bible words. He did this for two reasons: (1) he suspected that words not found in the Bible represented ideas not found there, and (2) things taught by God were better taught in the words which the Holy Spirit had chosen.[38] By "Bible

[34] Stone, *History of the Christian Church in the West*, pp. 6-17, 38.
[35] Alexander Campbell, *Memoirs of Elder Thomas Campbell* (Cincinnati, 1861), p. 28.
[36] Robert Richardson, *Memoirs of Alexander Campbell* (Cincinnati, 1897), I, 236.
[37] Alexander Campbell, "Sermon on the Law," *Biographies and Sermons of Pioneer Preachers*, ed. B. C. Goodpasture and W. T. Moore (Nashville, B. C. Goodpasture, 1954), pp. 5-9, 26-32.
[38] Campbell, *The Christian System*, p. 125.

words," Campbell meant English words, and did not indicate an awareness of the problem this involved. Although he knew Greek, he was willing to rely on the words of an English translation. He did not seem to realize that his position, to be consistent, would mean the use of Greek words and would involve him in all the problems of textual criticism.

Stone and Campbell agreed with O'Kelly that the Scriptures contained a pattern for church government, and they taught that this pattern was congregational. In his study of the Scriptures, Stone came to the conclusion that there was neither precept nor example in the New Testament for presbyteries, synods, and general assemblies. He and his co-workers, therefore, dissolved the Springfield Presbytery. In 1803, when Stone and four other Presbyterian ministers, Richard McNemar, John Thompson, John Dunlavy, and Robert Marshall, had incurred the displeasure of the Synod of Kentucky for preaching "anti-Calvinist doctrines," they withdrew from the Synod and formed the Springfield Presbytery. A year later, they decided to dissolve their organization and gave their reasons for so doing in a document entitled, "The Last Will and Testament of Springfield Presbytery." In this "Last Will and Testament," they gave up their power to make laws for the government of the church and to execute them by delegated authority. They willed that each local church resume her right of government, to try candidates for the ministry, to call her own preacher, to admit or remove members. They urged the church never again to delegate the right of government to any man or to any group of men.[39]

In Campbell's view, a local congregation was not under the jurisdiction of any other community of Christians. All congregations were equal and independent of one another.

---

[39] Stone, *Voices From Cane Ridge*, pp. 74-84. Also see Charles C. Ware, *Barton Warren Stone, Pathfinder of Christian Union* (St. Louis, 1932), pp. 124-143.

Campbell rejected synods and councils which shackled the minds of men.[40] He understood the term "bishop" to refer to an elder whose jurisdiction was limited to one congregation and was shared jointly with other elders.[41] Although churches were independent of each other, they were under obligation to co-operate with one another to promote the gospel.[42]

O'Kelly, Stone, and Campbell regarded their movements as reform movements. Christianity was in need of a reformation to restore the apostolic order. O'Kelly was attempting to "carry the ark back to its resting place." In his opinion, Luther and Calvin's Reformation was a great work, which yet remained far from the primitive order. It was so mixed with human corruption that in course of time the reformed churches became like their mother, Rome.[43]

Stone, too, considered his work a reformation. He dated the reformation from the time he and his followers rejected human creeds and party names and took the Bible alone.[44]

Campbell called his movement "the current reformation." [45] In the early days of the movement, he and his followers were called "Reformers." [46] Campbell, indeed, fully acknowledged that the world owed a debt to the Protestant Reformers. Luther had restored the Bible to the world and defied the arrogant pretensions of the tyrannical See of Rome. "But, unfortunately, at his death there was no Joshua to lead the people, who rallied under the banners of the Bible, out of the wilderness in which Luther died." The spirit of the Reformation was soon lost in the feuds of Protestant princes and rival po-

---

[40] Campbell, *The Christian System*, pp. 3, 73.
[41] *Millennial Harbinger*, ed. Alexander Campbell, 1830, pp. 427-428.
[42] Campbell, *The Christian System*, p. 73.
[43] O'Kelly, *The Prospect Before Us*, pp. 4-5, 69.
[44] Stone, *Voices From Cane Ridge*, p. 80.
[45] Campbell, *The Christian System*, p. 1.
[46] Winfred E. Garrison and Alfred T. DeGroot, *The Disciples of Christ, A History* (St. Louis, Christian Board of Publication, 1948), p. 162.

litical interests. Although Protestants hated the papacy, a secret lust for ecclesiastical power burned in the bosoms of Protestant popes. Creeds and manuals, synods and councils, and a worldly spirit soon quenched the fire of reform. Calvin revived the speculative theology of Augustine, and Geneva became the Alexandria of modern Europe. Extremes begot extremes. The works of merit of the Roman church drove Luther and Calvin to the extreme of "faith alone." Campbell approved of the judgment cited from Lord Chatham, that the Church of England was a singular compound: "A Popish liturgy, Calvinistic articles, and an Arminian clergy." In view of such abortive efforts to reform, Campbell sought to restore the ancient purity and peace of the church.[47]

O'Kelly, Stone, and Campbell hoped that their reformation would result in Christian unity. They attacked the evils of division and pointed out the desirability of unity. O'Kelly cited the example of the early church, which was of one heart and one mind. Divisions weakened Christ's spiritual army and cooled brotherly love. O'Kelly insisted that one faith was necessary for Christian unity. The New Testament commanded Christians to be of the same mind and to speak the same thing.[48] The reason why all should believe the one faith is that corrupt doctrine leads to divisions.[49] In seeking unity, O'Kelly could not accept the Baptist order, because "the door into their church is water."[50] He could not accept the Presbyterian order, because he could not acknowledge their Confession of Faith with its doctrine of predestination and election. He could not accept the Methodist order, because he would not submit to a human head, or to an oppressive and unscriptural form of government. O'Kelly proposed the following plan for Christian

---

[47] Campbell, *The Christian System*, pp. 3-5.
[48] O'Kelly, *The Divine Oracles Consulted*, pp. 3, 38, 52.
[49] O'Kelly, *Letters From Heaven Consulted*, p. 50.
[50] A reference to insistence by the Baptists on immersion for church membership.

union: (1) let the Presbyterians put aside their Confession of Faith and accept the Bible as sufficient for the faith and practice of the church, (2) let the Baptists admit to their communion all those of Christian life and experience, and (3) let the Methodists lay aside their book of discipline and follow the form of government given by the apostles. O'Kelly wanted Christ to be the only head of the church, her law, and her center of union.[51]

Stone denounced divisions and advocated the union of all Christians.[52] To him, sectarian debate of controversial opinions was a sign of the low state of religion. Human systems produced endless debates, cut up Christianity into hundreds of parties, and wasted strength in party conflicts.[53] Stone rejoiced in the revivals because they promoted unity; yet the revivals themselves were almost ruined by sectarian strife. Where there had been unity of doctrine and of spirit, the sticklers for Presbyterian orthodoxy injected their particular doctrines:

> The gauntlet was now thrown, and a fire was now kindled that threatened ruin to the great excitement; it revived the dying spirit of partyism, and gave life and strength to trembling infidels and lifeless professors. The sects were roused. The Methodists and Baptists, who had so long lived in peace and harmony with the Presbyterians, and with one another, now girded on their armor and marched into the deathly field of controversy and war. These were times of distress. The spirit of partyism soon expelled the spirit of love and union —peace fled before discord and strife, and religion was stifled and banished in the unhallowed struggle for preeminence.[54]

[51] O'Kelly, "A Plan of Union Proposed, etc.," *Herald of Gospel Liberty*, I (1808-1809), 39-40.
[52] Stone, *History of the Christian Church in the West*, p. 39.
[53] Stone, *Voices From Cane Ridge*, pp. 60, 121.
[54] *Ibid.*, p. 76.

Stone considered creeds the "very bane of Christian unity." [55]
Creeds and human forms of government were the principal
causes of divisions and party spirit.[56] His proposal for unity
was to unite in spirit on the Bible. He believed that bigotry
and party spirit were fast dying among Christians of all denominations, [57] and that one day the whole church would
unite on his principles.[58]

Campbell believed that the attainment of Christian unity
and the conversion of sinners were the greatest goals of life.
Christian unity was necessary for the conversion of the world,
for the combination of truth and unity would be sufficient
to convert the unbelieving nations. For unity to be achieved,
creeds must be discarded. Campbell maintained that no Protestant creed could be found which had not made a division
for every generation of its existence. To illustrate the divisive
effect of creeds, Campbell pointed to the different groups
which accepted the Westminster Confession in substance or
form: the General Assembly in Scotland and the United
States, the Cameronians or Solemn League and Covenant
Presbyterians, the Burghers or Unionists, the Anti-Burghers
or Seceders, the Relief Presbyterians, the Cumberland Presbyterians, and the New School Presbyterians. All of these originated from one creed; yet some were as "discordant and
aloof from each other as were the Jews and Samaritans." Although Campbell here cited the divisive effect of Protestant
creeds, he rejected the ancient Catholic creeds as well.[59] To
solve the problem of unity, he proposed the following plan:

> Let the BIBLE be substituted for all human
> creeds; FACTS, for definitions; THINGS, for words;
> FAITH, for speculation; UNITY OF FAITH, for

[55] Ibid., p. 78.
[56] Stone, History of the Christian Church in the West, pp. 39-40.
[57] Stone, Voices From Cane Ridge, pp. 101, 123.
[58] Stone, History of the Christian Church in the West, p. 49.
[59] Campbell, The Christian System, pp. 9, 107-109, 126.

> *unity of opinion;* THE POSITIVE COMMAND-
> MENTS OF GOD, *for human legislation and tradi-
> tion;* PIETY, *for ceremony,* MORALITY, *for par-
> tisan zeal;* THE PRACTICE OF RELIGION, *for the
> mere profession of it*: and the work is done.[60]

To promote unity and to demonstrate unity, O'Kelly, Stone,
and Campbell believed that sectarian names should be discarded and that believers should wear the name "Christian."
The use of different names contributed to division. O'Kelly
urged the rejection of all unscriptural names: "O why do we
wander in paths of *man's* invention, or cleave to the example
of *modern* churches; and why such violent attachment to
names—seeing, the royal standard is at hand?" [61] O'Kelly cited
the story of Paul before King Agrippa to show that in the
primitive church the disciples wore the name "Christian." It
should not be said that it does not matter what name is used.
Though names could not save, it was safe to follow the word.[62]
A believer glorified Christ when he bore the name "Christian." [63]

Stone and his co-workers gave up the name "Springfield
Presbytery," because it savored of a party spirit. They took
the name "Christian," which they believed to have been given
to the disciples by divine appointment first at Antioch. They
published a pamphlet, *An Address to the Different Religious
Societies on the Sacred Import of the Christian Name,* written
by Rice Haggard, who had recently united with Stone.[64]

Campbell also rejected sectarian names. His principles of
requiring a "Thus saith the Lord" for all practices, and of
expressing "Bible things by Bible words," when applied to

[60] *Ibid.,* p. 110.
[61] *Herald of Gospel Liberty,* I (1809), 44.
[62] O'Kelly, *The Divine Oracles Consulted,* p. 58.
[63] O'Kelly, *Letters From Heaven Consulted,* p. 52.
[64] Stone, *Voices From Cane Ridge,* p. 80.

the name of the church, meant that the church should be called either "Disciples of Christ" or "Christian." [65] Campbell preferred the former as more unassuming.[66]

Although O'Kelly, Stone, and Campbell agreed that creeds should be rejected and that the Scriptures should be used as the only guide to faith and practice, they disagreed on some points of scriptural exposition—on the doctrine of the Trinity, the doctrine of the Atonement, the nature of faith, and the doctrine of baptism.

O'Kelly taught that Jesus Christ was "equal deity" with the Father. Christ was God and God was Christ.[67] Arianism was false, because it taught that Jesus Christ was inferior to the Father. O'Kelly maintained that although the council of Nicea rejected Arianism, it established another new theology. This new theology, as O'Kelly understood it, taught that there were three *distinct* persons in the undivided Godhead! Yet as they say, the Father is God, Jesus is God, the Spirit is God— yet those persons are not three Gods—but *one* only!" O'Kelly believed that the only way the term "Trinity" could be used was to signify that all divine attributes resided in the one divine person, Jesus Christ. O'Kelly so emphasized the divinity of Christ that he emasculated his humanity. He denied that Christ had a human soul. Jesus Christ was God in the flesh, possessed of human feelings but with a divine soul.[68] O'Kelly's doctrine of the Trinity was thus a form of the ancient heresy of Apollinarius, Bishop of Laodicea in the second half of the fourth century. Apollinarius, using the threefold division of man, body, soul (animal soul or the principle of life), and spirit (rational soul), taught that Jesus Christ had a human

[65] The Acts of the Apostles 11:26.
[66] Alexander Campbell, *The Disciples of Christ* (Lexington, Ky., The College of the Bible, 1951), p. 6.
[67] O'Kelly, *The Prospect Before Us*, pp. 3-4, 18.
[68] O'Kelly, *The Divine Oracles Consulted*, pp. 29-31, 39-40.

body and animal soul, with the Logos taking the place of the spirit.[69]

Stone refused to use "unscriptural phraseology" in regard to the doctrine of the Trinity and wanted the doctrine expressed in the "language of the Holy Spirit, as taught in the Bible." He accepted the doctrine that "Jesus Christ was the Son of God, that he existed with the Father before creation, and was the agent by whom God made the world." Rejecting the terms "eternal Son" and "eternally begotten," Stone taught that the Father alone was eternal and that the Son had the status of a creature. Although he rejected the charge of Arianism, Stone was close to the Arian tradition.[70]

Campbell believed that the Father, Son, and Holy Spirit were "equally divine, though personally distinct from each other." There is one God, one Lord, one Holy Spirit, who are equally possessed of one and the same divine nature. The divine nature is essentially and necessarily singular but plural in its personal manifestations. Jesus was the Word of God made flesh. He who was supreme deity, became a true and proper man. Campbell believed that the eternal relation of Christ to the Godhead was as the Word and that his Sonship dated only from the Incarnation. In denying the eternal Sonship, Campbell departed from orthodox doctrine; nevertheless, he came closer to the orthodox position than either O'Kelly or Stone.[71]

O'Kelly held to a penal substitution theory of the Atone-

---

[69] Charles E. Raven, *Apollinarianism* (Cambridge, England, 1923), pp. 177-232. Also see James F. Bethune-Baker, *An Introduction to the Early History of Christian Doctrine* (London, Methuen and Co., Ltd., 1954), pp. 242-243.

[70] *Christian Messenger*, ed. Barton W. Stone, III (1829), 269-277. Also see William G. West, *Barton Warren Stone: Early American Advocate of Christian Unity* (Nashville, Disciples of Christ Historical Society, 1954), pp. 83-87.

[71] Campbell, *The Christian System*, pp. 20-23.

ment. Sin was the transgression of the law. Christ, the Holy One, became a sin-offering to appease divine justice. God could not countenance rebellion against His law. Christ, therefore, suffered the executive wrath of the law. The just suffered for the unjust. Only Christ's atoning blood could remove the guilt of sin. O'Kelly disagreed with Stone's interpretation of the Atonement. "Let Mr. Stone write on, and deny our Lord's penal sufferings, with his Greek phrase *at-one*, instead of *atone*; and what has he gained by that, only that God and man are at one or reconciled through the blood of his cross."[72]

On searching the Scriptures, Stone began to be troubled by the doctrine of the Atonement. He had believed that Christ died as a substitute for man and that he satisfied the demands of the law on man's behalf. Stone came to the conclusion that if this were true, either Universalism or the Calvinist doctrine of election and reprobation was true. Stone could not accept either as the doctrine of the Bible.[73] Furthermore, if Christ satisfied the demands of the law, then the sinner was freed from its obligations. This could not be true. Neither was it true that there was "surplus righteousness" in Christ's death which could be imputed to sinners for their justification. The expression, "imputed righteousness of Christ," was not found in the Bible.[74] The truth of the Atonement was found in the true spelling and pronunciation of the word, "at-one-ment." Sin had separated man from God. Christ restored the union or the "at-one-ment" between God and man. Stone was correct in this analysis of the word. Reconciliation took place when God saved a man from his sins and made him holy. The change was in man, not in God. Faith in Christ, who lived, died, and rose again, brought about the change.[75] Stone

[72] O'Kelly, *The Divine Oracles Consulted*, pp. 25-26, 43.
[73] Stone, *Voices From Cane Ridge*, p. 86.
[74] Stone, *History of the Christian Church in the West*, pp. 43-44.
[75] Stone, *Voices From Cane Ridge*, pp. 88-90.

thus understood the Scriptures to teach a moral theory of the Atonement; and Presbyterians, with some justification, attacked him for teaching unorthodox doctrines.[76]

Campbell's doctrine of the Atonement combined elements of the moral government and moral influence theories. Campbell used different words to present the different aspects of the Atonement: "Sacrifice, as respects *God*, is a propitiation; as respects *sinners*, it is a reconciliation; as respects *sin*, it is an expiation; as respects the *saved*, it is a redemption." The Atonement was the effect and not the cause of God's benevolence to sinners. But God could not ignore man's rebellion against His authority and government. He could not show mercy without sacrifice. However, the death of Jesus was not a payment of debt. His sacrifice was a moral, not a commercial transaction. If it were a payment of debt, justice would demand the release, not the pardon of the debtor. Christ's death effected a reconciliation between God and man. In regard to honor and justice, the death of Christ reconciled God to forgive; as a demonstration of love and mercy, it reconciled man to God.[77]

O'Kelly conceived of faith as brought about by the divine operation of the Holy Spirit, while Stone and Campbell had a more rationalistic view of faith. In describing his conversion, O'Kelly revealed his conception of how faith was produced in the sinner. His "first mental alarm" was not through preaching but through the "kind illuminations of the invisible Holy Spirit." Through this divine light, he saw that he was without God and without hope. He was moved to seek a place

---

[76] Thomas Cleland, *Letters to Barton W. Stone, Containing a Vindication Principally of the Doctrines of the Trinity, the Divinity and Atonement of the Saviour...* (Lexington, Ky., 1822) pp. 82-134. Also see Robert Davidson, *History of the Presbyterian Church in the State of Kentucky* (New York, 1847), pp. 190-222.

[77] Campbell, *The Christian System*, pp. 35-38.

of refuge.[78] In the creation of faith, O'Kelly did not exclude preaching; but he emphasized the role of the Holy Spirit.[79]

To Stone, faith was believing the testimony of God given in the Scriptures. There was sufficient evidence in the word to produce faith, and the sinner was capable of believing. Faith did not depend on holiness but on the strength of the testimony. God had provided the means of salvation in the preaching of the gospel; the sinner was to use the means.[80] The sinner did not need to go through a long period of anguish, waiting for the Holy Spirit to come. God gave the Spirit after the sinner believed. He did not have to wait, only to believe.[81]

Campbell agreed with Stone that faith was the belief of testimony. Any man was capable of faith simply by studying the evidence given in Scripture. The evidence produced faith in Jesus as the Messiah.[82] Campbell did not believe that an evangelist should try to induce a mystical state giving rise to an "assurance of pardon." He objected to calling upon the Holy Spirit to bestow saving faith on a mourning sinner, and to emotional techniques, such as giving vivid pictures of the fate of the damned. Rather, the evangelist should intelligently present the evidence for the Messiahship of Jesus.[83] Campbell, as well as Stone, came close to a rationalistic definition of faith. They failed to take into account the teaching of the apostle Paul that "no man can say that Jesus is the Lord, but by the Holy Spirit." [84]

O'Kelly differed with Stone and Campbell on the doctrine of baptism. O'Kelly believed in infant baptism and sprinkling,

[78] O'Kelly, "My Conversion," in Barrett, *Centennial of Religious Journalism*, p. 252.
[79] O'Kelly, *Letters From Heaven Consulted*, p. 50.
[80] Stone, *History of the Christian Church in the West*, pp. 27, 33-34.
[81] Stone, *Voices From Cane Ridge*, pp. 41, 75.
[82] Campbell, *The Christian System*, pp. 113-122.
[83] *Millennial Harbinger*, 1840, pp. 167-168.
[84] I Corinthians 12:3.

while Stone and Campbell advocated believer's baptism and immersion. In an effort to prove that children were proper subjects of baptism, O'Kelly quoted Mark 10:14, "Suffer the little children to come unto me, and forbid them not; for of such is the kingdom of God." The children of Christian people should have a visible seal of the covenant as Jewish children had by circumcision. It was right to baptize children even if one parent was an unbeliever. The Christian parent sanctified the unbelieving partner in a "federal sense" and thus made the children proper subjects. Baptism was a privilege and a national right for children who were born in Christendom. To deprive them of baptism was to rob them of their birthright. By means of infant baptism, nations had been civilized and Christianized.[85] O'Kelly did not believe that the accounts of conversion in the Acts of the Apostles supported the practice of immersion. He doubted that the three thousand converts on the day of Pentecost had to give an account of their experience, one by one, and were then marched to a certain water to be dipped, either in their clothes or naked.[86] Concerning the baptism of the jailer and his family, O'Kelly observed:

> If any man in his senses can believe that the family were carried, at that hour, through guards and gates, in the dark or with lamps, (the city alarmed) to a suitable water, with garments on or naked, were dipped, and went back through all, undiscovered—and Paul also, to play the hypocrite, even refuse to go out in the morning: to believe in the doctrine of immersion from this report, is to read one way and believe another.[87]

In O'Kelly's opinion, water baptism in any mode was not

[85] O'Kelly, *The Prospect Before Us*, pp. 12-14.
[86] O'Kelly, *The Divine Oracles Consulted*, pp. 46-47.
[87] *Ibid.*, p. 53.

essential. It was only an outward sign of the inner, spiritual baptism.[88] In teaching infant baptism, O'Kelly departed from the usual practice of groups seeking the restoration of "primitive Christianity," for such groups generally insist on believer's baptism.[89]

From reading the Bible, Stone became convinced that immersion was the apostolic mode of baptism, and that believers were the only proper subjects.[90] Baptism was ordained for the remission of sins. Stone came to the conclusion that the command of the apostle Peter, "Repent, and be baptized every one of you in the name of Jesus Christ for the remission of sins, and ye shall receive the gift of the Holy Ghost," was the proper admonition to give to penitent sinners.[91] He credited Campbell with leading him into a fuller understanding of this doctrine.[92] Some of Stone's co-workers did not agree with him on believer's baptism; so they decided that each individual could act according to his conviction. They sought to avoid controversy on the subject and instructed the people to turn to the New Testament for guidance. In point of fact, most of Stone's group submitted to re-baptism by immersion.[93]

Campbell believed that the only proper subjects of baptism were those who had heard the gospel and believed. He based his position on Mark 16:16, "He that believeth and is baptized shall be saved." This divinely given sequence of faith followed by baptism should not be changed. The record of conversions in the Acts of the Apostles showed that the baptism of those who heard and believed was the "uniform and immutable practice during the apostolic age." Immersion was

[88] O'Kelly, *Letters From Heaven Consulted*, p. 31.
[89] Alfred T. DeGroot, *The Restoration Principle* (St. Louis, The Bethany Press, 1960), pp. 99, 120, 150.
[90] Stone, *History of the Christian Church in the West*, p. 47.
[91] The Acts of the Apostles 2:38.
[92] Stone, *Voices From Cane Ridge*, p. 91.
[93] Stone, *History of the Christian Church in the West*, p. 47.

the only proper mode of baptism.[94] Campbell attached great importance to this rite. A sinner received the remission of his sins in the "very instant" of immersion.[95] Baptism, therefore, vitally affected the spiritual condition of the subject and should not be considered a "mere ceremonial introduction" into the church.[96]

In view of the conflicting opinions among the three men, the question arises as to whether Stone was justly called a "deserter" when he joined forces with Campbell. The answer is found in the nature of the union between O'Kelly's group and Stone's group, and in Stone's attitude toward his union with Campbell. The union between O'Kelly's followers and Stone's was not an official, organic church union. It was rather an unofficial recognition of "oneness," of similarity of doctrinal views. This feeling of brotherhood was expressed by the movement of preachers from one group to the other. Stone recorded that three elders who had left the Methodist Church with O'Kelly had united with him.[97] Guirey reported in the *Herald of Gospel Liberty* that those in Kentucky who had separated from the Presbyterians had united with O'Kelly's church.[98] The two groups shared a common bond of a desire to return to New Testament Christianity. Each group continued to work in its own area, looking upon the other as engaged in the same task.

When Stone had the opportunity of uniting with Campbell, he considered it a means of furthering his cherished ideal of unity. The union came about when the "Reforming Baptists" and the "Christians" in Georgetown, Kentucky, agreed to meet and worship together. They found they were of the

[94] Alexander Campbell, *Christian Baptism* (Nashville, Gospel Advocate Co., 1951), pp. 85, 176, 182.
[95] *The Christian Baptist*, ed. Alexander Campbell (7 vols. in one, Cincinnati, 1870). p. 417.
[96] Campbell, *Christian Baptism*, p. 206.
[97] Stone, *History of the Christian Church in the West*, p. 42.
[98] *Herald of Gospel Liberty*, I (1808-1809), 43.

same spirit, were built on the same foundation, and bore
the same name. They saw no reason why they should not be
the same family. Consequently, in Georgetown in December,
1831, and in Lexington in January, 1832, they had joint four-
day meetings, which they regarded as the beginning of union
between the two groups.[99] Stone at first had felt that there
were doctrinal differences in regard to baptism for the remission of sins, weekly communion, and the influence of the
Holy Spirit in conversion. After discussing the issues with
the "Reformers," he concluded that his views and theirs were
one.[100] They agreed to allow differences of opinion as long
as they were not imposed on others as articles of faith. The
only creed or confession which was to serve as a common
bond of union was to be the New Testament. To them, the
New Testament was a perfect creed, delivered from heaven,
and confirmed by Jesus and the Apostles. The two groups
decided to build up churches without regard to their former
names. To consolidate the union, they appointed John Smith
(Reformer), and John Rogers (Christian) to travel among
the churches. They were to be supported by contributions from
both churches.[101] As a further mark of unity, John T. Johnson became co-editor of Stone's paper, the *Christian Messenger*. The union was easily accomplished in Kentucky. It
would have taken place as easily in other states, according
to Stone, had it not been for a "few ignorant, headstrong big-
ots on both sides, who were more influenced to retain and
augment their party, than to save the world by uniting according to the prayer of Jesus." [102]

Stone was criticized by O'Kelly's group for uniting with
Campbell, but Stone considered the union "the noblest act"
of his life:

[99] Stone, *History of the Christian Church in the West*, p. 51.
[100] Stone, *Voices From Cane Ridge*, p. 107.
[101] Stone, *History of the Christian Church in the West*, pp. 51-52.
[102] Stone, *Voices From Cane Ridge*, p. 108.

It is not wonderful that the prejudices of the old Christian church should be great against us, and that they should so unkindly upbraid me especially, and my brethren in Kentucky, for uniting with the Reformers. But what else could we do, the Bible being our directory? Should we command them to leave the foundation on which we stood —the Bible alone— when they had come upon the same? By what authority could we command? Or should we have left this foundation to them, and have built another? Or should we have remained, and fought with them for the sole possession? They held the name *Christian* as sacred as we did —they were equally averse from making opinions the test of fellowship— and equally solicitous for the salvation of souls. This union, irrespective of reproach, I view as the noblest act of my life.[103]

Stone was determined to do what he believed to be right, regardless of what others thought or did.

What was the relationship of the resultant Stone-Campbell movement with O'Kelly's church? O'Kelly, Stone, and Campbell were agreed that Calvinism was contrary to the Scriptures and that Christian perfection was a scriptural doctrine. They believed that the primitive church was the standard for the church of all ages. Rejecting creeds, they took the New Testament as their only rule of faith and practice. They understood the New Testament to teach a congregational form of church government. Their movements were "reform" movements which would finish the work of the Reformation and would result in Christian unity. They chose the name "Christian" as the name which all disciples should wear. They disagreed, however, on the doctrine of the Trinity, the doctrine of the Atonement, the nature of faith, and the doctrine of baptism. Stone agreed with Campbell, rather than with O'Kelly, on the nature of faith and the doctrine of baptism. Stone's

103 *Ibid.*, p. 109.

doctrine of the Atonement was closer to Campbell's than to O'Kelly's. Stone was thus closer doctrinally to Campbell than to O'Kelly.

In conclusion, O'Kelly was a leader of a movement similar to that of Stone and Campbell. Although O'Kelly differed on some specific points of doctrine, he had the same goal of restoring the primitive church by using the New Testament as the only rule of faith and practice. In leaving the Methodist Episcopal Church, O'Kelly believed that he was leaving a church with an unscriptural and oppressive government. He intended to establish a church which would faithfully follow the "apostolic order." The problem remains, however, as to what constitutes the "apostolic order." The doctrinal differences between O'Kelly, Stone, and Campbell show the difficulty of the restoration principle. All three men agreed that there was "one faith" which the Lord had given to the early church and which He intended to be the faith of the church in all ages. They agreed that the New Testament should be the only rule of faith and practice. The difficulty came when they put this rule into practice. What is the "one faith"? What church order does the New Testament give? The New Testament supposedly gives a clear pattern; yet the three men disagreed on the pattern. This is seen, for example, in the doctrine of baptism. O'Kelly firmly believed that the New Testament authorized infant baptism and sprinkling, while Stone and Campbell believed just as firmly in believer's baptism and immersion. The problem is further illustrated by Asbury's conviction that the itinerant episcopacy was apostolic, while O'Kelly, Stone, and Campbell believed that the New Testament clearly revealed a congregational form of government. The doctrinal differences also show that the restoration of the primitive church is not an easy path to Christian unity.

Although the three men rejected creeds so that they might be free to follow the Scriptures, they had their own conception of what the Scriptures taught, which amounted to an unwritten creed. O'Kelly sought freedom from ecclesiastical control, but he did not thereby intend that everyone should be free to believe as he chose. Every Christian was under obligation to receive the "faith once delivered to the saints." Although O'Kelly's movement and the Stone-Campbell movement ultimately went separate ways, in their early days they were expressions of a common search for the unity and purity of the primitive church.

SOURCES FOR THE STUDY OF O'KELLY

Although James O'Kelly's works are rare and difficult to secure, the most important ones are extant and make a study of the schism possible. The *Apology for Protesting Against the Methodist Episcopal Government* (Hillsboro, N. C., 1829)[1] contains a brief account of the controversies which preceded the General Conference in 1792, the events at the Conference, and the separation which followed. As the title indicates, O'Kelly's main purpose in this work is to attack the episcopal form of government. O'Kelly's only known writing which preceded his break with Methodism is his *Essay on Negro-Slavery* (Philadelphia, 1789), in which he uses both Scripture and the Philosophy of Natural Rights to attack slavery. O'Kelly wrote two commentaries, *The Divine Oracles Consulted* (Hillsboro, N. C., 1820), which treats Matthew, Mark, Luke, John, and the Acts of the Apostles; and *Letters From Heaven Consulted* (Hillsboro, N. C., 1822), a commentary on Romans through Revelation. These are not systematic studies. O'Kelly often skips entire chapters and sometimes devotes as little as one paragraph to a book (e.g., the Gospel of Mark). He centers his attention on passages which afford him an opportunity to expound his views on church government, Calvinism, the divin-

---

[1] This is the date of the copy used in this study. The *Apology* was first published about 1798, as Snethen's *Reply to an Apology* was published in 1800.

ity of Christ, and baptism. O'Kelly compiled a hymnal for his
denomination's use, *Hymns and Spiritual Songs, Designed for
the Use of Christians* (Raleigh, N. C., 1816). In the preface he
says that he wrote some of the hymns; but he does not indicate
which ones, as no authors are given. The hymnal is important,
for devotional material reveals much about doctrinal beliefs.
Two years before his death, O'Kelly wrote *The Prospect Before
Us, By Way of Address to the Christian Church* (Hillsboro,
N. C., 1824). He only devotes five pages, however, to the prospect before his church, while in the remainder of the work he
deals with the "apostolic order," and the divinity of Christ, and
attacks the Baptists in regard to the doctrine of baptism. O'Kelly
gave his plan for Christian unity in "A Plan of Union Proposed, etc.," published in the *Herald of Gospel Liberty*, I (1808-
1809). A one page account of his conversion, entitled simply
"My Conversion," is printed in the *Centennial of Religious
Journalism* (Dayton, Ohio, 1908), edited by John P. Barrett,
but the original source is not given. In a letter addressed to a
"dear brother," O'Kelly gives his objections to Wesley's appointment of Richard Whatcoat as superintendent. This letter
is printed in the *Journal and Letters of Francis Asbury* (Nashville, 1958), III, 47-53. In two other letters, written shortly
after the General Conference of 1792, O'Kelly defends his
separation from the Methodists. These are printed in William
W. Bennett, *Memorials of Methodism in Virginia* (Richmond,
1871), pp. 323-326.

The foregoing works were consulted in the preparation of
the present study. Claude Spencer's *An Author Catalog of Disciples of Christ and Related Groups* (Canton, Missouri, 1946)
lists several additional titles which, despite an extensive search,
could not be located: *Annotation of His Book of Discipline*
(1809), *The Christian Church* (1801), *Christicola, Church Government, Commentaries on the Books of the New Testament,
A Tract on Baptism,* and *A Vindication of an Apology* (1801).

Some of these titles may be duplications. For example, *Commentaries on the Books of the New Testament* may refer to *The Divine Oracles Consulted* and *Letters From Heaven Consulted*. "Christicola" was the pen name which O'Kelly used for his *Apology*, and the title *Christicola* may refer to this work. The title, *Annotation of His Book of Discipline*, does not ring true with O'Kelly, since he rejected disciplines and creeds and professed to follow only the Scriptures. Although O'Kelly's *Vindication of an Apology* was not located, its subject matter is easily ascertained from Nicholas Snethen's *An Answer to James O'Kelly's Vindication of His Apology*. The subject matter of three works, *Church Government*, *A Tract on Baptism*, and *The Christian Church* is found in other works: his conception of church government and his doctrine of the church in the *Apology*, and his doctrine of baptism in *The Prospect Before Us*.

The standard biography of O'Kelly is Wilbur E. MacClenny's *The Life of Rev. James O'Kelly* (Raleigh, N. C., 1910). This is a partisan defense of O'Kelly and lacks objectivity. Although he uses O'Kelly's *Apology*, MacClenny leans heavily on secondary sources, such as Edward J. Drinkhouse's *History of Methodist Reform* (2 vols., Baltimore, 1899). Biographical sketches of O'Kelly are found in Matthew H. Moore, *Sketches of the Pioneers of Methodism in North Carolina and Virginia* (Nashville, 1884), Peter J. Kernodle, *Lives of Christian Ministers* (Richmond, 1909), and Milo T. Morrill, *A History of the Christian Denomination* (Dayton, Ohio, 1912). Kernodle uses more original sources than does MacClenny, whereas Morrill depends heavily on MacClenny's work. Moore includes O'Kelly among the Methodist pioneers and tries to present him in a fair light.

Most of the works which deal with O'Kelly are denominational histories which are written from a filial viewpoint, either in praise or in condemnation. The historians of O'Kelly's own denomination praise him as a champion of liberty. In the *Centennial of Religious Journalism* (Dayton, Ohio, 1908), edited by John P. Barrett, O'Kelly is presented as one who fought prejudice, ignorance, and sectarian bias, and was a prophet of a broader fellowship among Christians. Milo T. Morrill, *A History of the Christian Denomination in America* (Dayton, Ohio, 1912), describes the O'Kelly schism as a struggle between a liberty-loving patriot and an autocratic hierarchy; and John F. Burnett, *Rev. James O'Kelly: A Champion of Religious Liberty* (Dayton, Ohio, n. d.), depicts O'Kelly as a Christian democrat, a moral hero, and a pioneer of Christian liberty who fought against the autocratic spirit of the Methodist Church. William A. Harper, *The Genius of the Christian Church* (Elon College, N. C., 1929), says that O'Kelly's movement was an effort to reproduce in the life of the church the pattern of American democracy, establishing thereby a free church, governed by free believers, in a free country. In the *Christian Denomination and Christian Doctrine* (Dayton, Ohio, n.d.), Simon A. Bennett claims that O'Kelly stood for liberty and individualism and that his movement was motivated by a desire for freedom of mind and expression.

Methodist historians in general have represented the O'Kelly controversy as (1) an unjust attack on Asbury, (2) a needless strife which interfered with the progress of the church, and (3) the establishment of a denomination which soon declined in numbers and influence. Abel Stevens, *History of the Methodist Episcopal Church* (New York, 1867), defends the episcopacy against O'Kelly's attack and states that submission to the episcopacy is heroism and not servility. He says that in the early years O'Kelly was highly esteemed for his talent and devotion, but that he used unjustifiable methods in drawing away members from the Methodist Episcopal Church. In *Memorials of Methodism in Virginia* (Richmond, 1871),

William W. Bennett strongly condemns O'Kelly, calling him a heretic who was motivated by ambition, was determined to rule or ruin the church, and whose schemes ended in failure. Matthew Simpson, *A Hundred Years of Methodism* (New York, 1876), says that O'Kelly severely assailed Asbury, retarded the progress of the Methodist Episcopal Church, and enjoyed only a temporary success. Holland N. McTyeire, *A History of Methodism* (Nashville, 1889), concludes that there is no evidence that O'Kelly was guilty of heresy, but calls him an "arch-agitator" who sowed discord and strife among the Methodists and lived to see his own movement scattered and broken into contending factions. James M. Buckley, however, in *A History of Methodists in the United States* (American Church History Series, V, New York, 1897), claims that O'Kelly preached heretical doctrines, but he agrees with McTyeire that O'Kelly's movement divided and subdivided. John F. Hurst, *The History of Methodism* (New York, 1902), gives a more dispassionate account of the schism, noting the temporary loss suffered by the Methodists and the eventual decline of O'Kelly's denomination. Halford E. Luccock and Paul Hutchinson, *The Story of Methodism* (New York, 1927), are more sympathetic towards O'Kelly and conclude that the division was a result of the spirit of the times rather than of any defect in O'Kelly's character.

Contemporary sources, in addition to O'Kelly's works, include Francis Asbury's *Journal and Letters* (3 vols., Nashville, 1958). His *Journal*, however, does not contain as much detailed information about the controversies as might be expected as Asbury says as little as possible about a subject which was extremely unpleasant to him. *The Causes, Evils, and Cures of Heart and Church Divisions* (Nashville, 1875), edited by Asbury, is a good source for Asbury's doctrine of the church and his attitude toward the problem of division. Jesse Lee's *Short History of the Methodists* (Baltimore, 1810), although written from a partisan Methodist viewpoint, provides much source material. The same is true of William Guirey's *History of Episcopacy* (n.p., n.d.), written from the opposing viewpoint. Guirey was a Methodist preacher who joined O'Kelly's movement. *Minutes of Several Conversations between the Rev. Thomas Coke, LL. D., the Rev. Francis Asbury and Others, 1784.* . . . and succeeding editions of the *Discipline* though 1796 are valuable for ascertaining the structure of the Methodist Episcopal Church during this period. The *Disciplines* are especially helpful if consulted in connection with Robert Emory's *History of the Discipline of the Methodist Episcopal Church* (New York, 1844). Asbury and Coke's "Notes on the Discipline," printed in Emory, are useful in understanding the Methodist defense against O'Kelly. The *Minutes* of the conferences are disappointingly brief and give few details about the controversy. Nicholas Snethen, using materials gathered by Asbury, wrote the official Methodist *Reply to an Apology* (Philadelphia, 1800). When O'Kelly wrote *A Vindication of an Apology*, Snethen followed it with an *Answer to James O'Kelly's Vindication of His Apology* (Philadelphia, 1802).

A good study of Methodist dissent is Edward J. Drinkhouse's *History of Methodist Reform* (2 vols., Baltimore, 1899), but this must be used carefully, as Drinkhouse wrote from the viewpoint of the Methodist Protestant Church. Another good secondary work, although slanted toward the Methodist viewpoint, is William W. Sweet's *Virginia Methodism, A History* (Richmond, 1955). Winfred E. Garrison and Alfred T. DeGroot devote a short section to O'Kelly in their *Disciples of Christ, A History* (St. Louis, 1948).

Although O'Kelly's works are rare and primary biographical material is almost non-existent, there are sufficient primary sources available to make scholarly studies of the schism possible.

BIBLIOGRAPHY

I. PRIMARY WORKS

A. BOOKS

Asbury, Francis. *The Causes, Evils, and Cures of Heart and Church Divisions.* Nashville, 1875.

——. *The Journal and Letters of Francis Asbury,* ed. Elmer T. Clark. 3 vols., Nashville (Abingdon Press), 1958.

Campbell, Alexander. *Christian Baptism.* Nashville (Gospel Advocate Co.), 1951.

——. *The Christian System. Cincinnati* (Standard Publishing Co.), n.d.

——. *The Disciples of Christ.* Lexington, Ky. (The College of the Bible), 1951.

——. *Memoirs of Elder Thomas Campbell.* Cincinnati, 1861.

——. "Sermon on the Law." *Biographies and Sermons of Pioneer Preachers,* ed. B. C. Goodpasture and W. T. Moore. Nashville (B. C. Goodpasture), 1954, pp. 1-32.

Cleland, Thomas. *Letters to Barton W. Stone, Containing a Vindication Principally of the Doctrines of the Trinity, the Divinity and Atonement of the Saviour....* Lexington, Ky., 1822.

Guirey, William. *The History of Episcopacy in Four Parts, From Its Rise to the Present Day.* n.p., n.d.

Haggard, Rice. *An Address to the Different Religious Societies on the Sacred Import of the Christian Name.* Nashville (Disciples of Christ Historical Society), 1954.

Jefferson, Thomas. "The Declaration of Independence." *We Hold These Truths,* ed. Stuart G. Brown. New York (Harper), 1941.

Journal of the General Conference of the Methodist Episcopal Church, 1792. Cincinnati, 1899.

Lee, Jesse. *A Short History of the Methodists, in the United States of America.* Baltimore, 1810

Locke, John. *Two Treatises of Government.* New York (Hafner), 1947.

Minutes of the Annual Conferences of the Methodist Episcopal Church, 1773-1828. New York, 1840.

Minutes of Several Conversations between the Rev. Thomas Coke, LL. D., the Rev. Francis Asbury and others.... Philadelphia, 1784-1796.

O'Kelly, James. *The Author's Apology for Protesting Against the Methodist Episcopal Government.* Hillsboro, N. C., 1829.

——. *The Divine Oracles Consulted: Or an Appeal to the Law and Testimony.* Hillsboro, N. C., 1820.

——. *Essay on Negro-Slavery.* Philadelphia, 1789.

——. *Hymns and Spiritual Songs, Designed for the Use of Christians.* Raleigh, 1816.

——. Letter to a "dear brother." *Journal and Letters of Francis Asbury,* ed. Elmer T. Clark. Nashville (Abingdon Press), 1958, III, 47-53.

——. Letters to Jesse Nicholson and Colonel Williams. William W. Bennett, *Memorials of Methodism in Virginia.* Richmond, 1871, pp. 323-326.

——. *Letters From Heaven Consulted.* Hillsboro, N. C., 1822.

——. "My Conversion." *The Centennial of Religious Journalism,* ed. John P. Barrett. Dayton, Ohio, 1908.

——. "A Plan of Union Proposed, etc." *Herald of Gospel Liberty,* I (1808-1809), 39-40, 43-44.

——. *The Prospect Before Us. By Way of Address to the Christian Church.* Hillsboro, N. C., 1824.

Paine, Thomas. *Selections from The Works of Thomas Paine.* New York, 1928.

Snethen, Nicholas. *An Answer to James O'Kelly's Vindication of His Apology, etc. and an Explanation of the Reply.* Philadelphia, 1802.

——. *A Reply to an Apology for Protesting Against the Methodist Episcopal Government.* Philadelphia, 1800.

Stone, Barton W. "A Short History of the Life of Barton W. Stone, written by Himself." *Voices from Cane Ridge,* ed. Rhodes Thompson. St. Louis (The Bethany Press), 1954, pp. 29-109.

——. *History of the Christian Church in the West.* Lexington, Ky. (The College of the Bible), 1956.

U. S. Department of Commerce, Bureau of the Census. *Religious Bodies: 1926.* 2 vols., Washington, 1929.

Ware, Thomas. *Sketches of the Life and Travels of Rev. Thomas Ware.* New York, 1840.

Wesley, John. *The Letters of the Rev. John Wesley, A. M.,* ed. John Telford. 8 vols., London, 1931.

——. *Wesley's Standard Sermons,* ed. Edward H. Sugden. 2 vols., London (The Epworth Press), 1956.

——. *The Works of the Rev. John Wesley, A. M.* 15 vols., London, 1866.

B. PERIODICALS

Christian Baptist, ed. Alexander Campbell. 7 vols. in one, Cincinnati, 1870.

Christian Messenger, ed. Barton W. Stone and others. 14 vols., Georgetown, Ky., and Jacksonville, Ill., 1826-1845.

Herald of Gospel Liberty, ed. Elias Smith and others. 122 vols., Portsmouth, N. H., 1808-1930.

Millennial Harbinger, ed. Alexander Campbell. 35 vols., Bethany, Va., 1830-1864.

II. SECONDARY WORKS

Barrett, John P., ed. *The Centennial of Religious Journalism.* Dayton, Ohio, 1908.

Bennett, Simon A. *The Christian Denomination and Christian Doctrine.* Dayton, Ohio, n.d.

Bennett, William W. *Memorials of Methodism in Virginia.* Richmond, 1871.

Bethune-Baker, James F. *An Introduction to the Early History of Christian Doctrine.* London (Methuen and Co., Ltd.), 1954.

Billington, Ray A. *The Protestant Crusade, 1800-1860.* New York (Rinehart and Company), 1952.

Brown, Stuart G. *The First Republicans.* Syracuse (Syracuse University Press), 1954.

Buckley, James M. *A History of Methodists in the United States.* American Church History Series, V. New York, 1897.

Burnett, John F. *Rev. James O'Kelly, A Champion of Religious Liberty.* Dayton, Ohio, n.d.

Cragg, Gerald R. *From Puritanism to the Age of Reason.* Cambridge (University Press), 1950.

Cross, Arthur L. *The Anglican Episcopate and the American Colonies.* New York, 1902.

Curti, Merle. *The Growth of American Thought.* New York (Harper), 1951.

Davidson, Robert. *History of the Presbyterian Church in the State of Kentucky.* New York, 1847.

DeGroot, Alfred T. *The Restoration Principle.* St. Louis (The Bethany Press), 1960.

Dictionary of American Biography. 22 vols., New York (Charles Scribner's Sons), 1928-1958.

Drinkhouse, Edward J. *History of Methodist Reform*. 2 vols., Baltimore, 1899.

Emory, Robert. *History of the Discipline of the Methodist Episcopal Church*. New York, 1844.

Faulkner, John A. *Burning Questions in Historic Christianity*. New York, 1930.

Garrison, Winfred E. and Alfred T. DeGroot. *The Disciples of Christ, A History*. St. Louis (The Bethany Press), 1948.

Harper, William A. *The Genius of the Christian Church*. Elon College, N. C., 1929.

Hurst, John F. *The History of Methodism*. New York, 1902.

Kernodle, Peter J. *Lives of Christian Ministers*. Richmond, 1909.

Landis, Benson Y., ed. *Yearbook of American Churches, 1959*. New York (National Council of the Churches of Christ in the U. S. A.), 1959.

Lawson, John. *Methodism and Catholicism*. London (S.P.C.K.), 1954.

Littell, Franklin H. *The Anabaptist View of the Church*. Boston (Starr King Press), 1958.

Luccock, Halford E. and Paul Hutchinson. *The Story of Methodism*. New York, 1926.

MacClenny, Wilbur E. *The Life of Rev. James O'Kelly*. Indianapolis (Religious Book Service), 1950.

McTyeire, Holland N. *A History of Methodism*. Nashville, 1889.

Mode, Peter G. *The Frontier Spirit in American Christianity*. New York, 1923.

Moore, Matthew H. *Sketches of the Pioneers of Methodism in North Carolina and Virginia*. Nashville, 1884.

Morrill, Milo T. *A History of the Christian Denomination in America*. Dayton, Ohio, 1912.

Paine, Robert. *Life and Times of William McKendree*. 2 vols., Nashville, 1869.

Raven, Charles E. *Apollinarianism*. Cambridge, England, 1923.

Richardson, Robert. *Memoirs of Alexander Campbell*. 2 vols., Cincinnati, 1897.

Simpson, Matthew. *A Hundred Years of Methodism*. New York, 1876.

Spencer, Claude E. *An Author Catalog of Disciples of Christ and Related Religious Groups*. Canton, Mo. (Disciples of Christ Historical Society), 1946.

Stevens, Abel. *History of the Methodist Episcopal Church in the United States of America*. 3 vols., New York, 1867.

Streeter, Burnett H. *The Primitive Church*. New York, 1929.

Sweet, William W. *American Culture and Religion*. Dallas (SMU Press),
    1951.
——. *Methodism in American History*. New York, 1933.
——. *Virginia Methodism, A History*. Richmond (Whittet and Shepper-
    son), 1955.
Tigert, John J. *A Constitutional History of American Episcopal Method-
    ism*. Nashville, 1904.
Ware, Charles C. *Barton Warren Stone, Pathfinder of Christian Union*.
    St. Louis, 1932.
West, Earl. *The Search for the Ancient Order*. 2 vols., Nashville (Gospel
    Advocate Co.), 1949.
West, William G. *Barton Warren Stone: Early American Advocate of
    Christian Unity*. Nashville (Disciples of Christ Historical Society),
    1954.

Este libro se acabó de imprimir el
día 30 de Mayo de 1963, en los ta-
lleres de Impresora GALVE, S. A.,
Callejón de San Antonio Abad 39,
de la ciudad de México.
El tiraje fue de 1,000 ejemplares.